"This work is a refreshing and concise account of the development of corporate governance. It offers a fascinating and coherent explanation of the complexities of governance, and a robust critique of dominant ideologies. The book highlights the imperative of the transformation from maximising shareholder value to sustainable value creation."

—**Wafa Khlif**, *University of Toulouse*
Business School, France

Comparative Corporate Governance

Corporate governance developed to maintain the accountability, stability, and performance of corporations. It has evolved to concern not just the financial health of the company, but its social and environmental impact. There is considerable international institutional diversity in corporate governance. The role and significance of market institutions varies among different governance systems.

This work provides a concise insight into the defining impulses of late twentieth- and early twenty-first-century corporate governance evolving through a series of competing epoch-making paradigmatic contests. The present paradigm highlights a shift towards corporate sustainability involving the corporate delivery of long-term value in financial, social, environmental, and ethical terms. In analysing the purpose of the company and the definition of value creation, the hegemony of agency theory and shareholder primacy is challenged. More expansive theoretical explanations are considered which recognise the deeper values companies are built upon, the wider purposes they serve, and the broader set of relationships they depend upon for their success.

This book will be of value to researchers, scholars, and students in corporate governance, sustainability, business, and accounting. Managers, professionals, and other general business readers will also find this text of interest.

Thomas Clarke is a Fellow of the Royal Society of Arts, Visiting Professor at Toulouse Business School (Barcelona), and was a Foundation Professor at the China Europe International Business School (CEIBS).

State of the Art in Business Research
Series Editor: Geoffrey Wood

Recent advances in theory, methods and applied knowledge (alongside structural changes in the global economic ecosystem) have presented researchers with challenges in seeking to stay abreast of their fields and navigate new scholarly terrains.

State of the Art in Business Research presents shortform books which provide an expert map to guide readers through new and rapidly evolving areas of research. Each title will provide an overview of the area, a guide to the key literature and theories and time-saving summaries of how theory interacts with practice.

As a collection, these books provide a library of theoretical and conceptual insights, and exposure to novel research tools and applied knowledge, that aid and facilitate in defining the state of the art, as a foundation stone for a new generation of research.

Organization Theory
A Research Overview
Gibson Burrell

Healthcare Management Control
A Research Overview
Michelle Carr and Matthias Beck

Comparative Corporate Governance
A Research Overview
Thomas Clarke

For more information about this series, please visit: www.routledge.com/State-of-the-Art-in-Business-Research/book-series/START

Comparative Corporate Governance

A Research Overview

Thomas Clarke

Routledge
Taylor & Francis Group

LONDON AND NEW YORK

First published 2023
by Routledge
4 Park Square, Milton Park, Abingdon, Oxon OX14 4RN

and by Routledge
605 Third Avenue, New York, NY 10158

Routledge is an imprint of the Taylor & Francis Group, an informa business

© 2023 Thomas Clarke

British Library Cataloguing-in-Publication Data
A catalogue record for this book is available from the British Library

Library of Congress Cataloging-in-Publication Data
Names: Clarke, Thomas, 1950- author.
Title: Comparative corporate governance: a research overview /
Thomas Clarke.
Description: 1 Edition. | New York, NY: Routledge, 2023. | Series: State
of the art in business research | Includes bibliographical references
and index.
Identifiers: LCCN 2022014410 (print) | LCCN 2022014411 (ebook)
Subjects: LCSH: Corporate governance. | Social responsibility of business.
Classification: LCC HD2741.C5673 2023 (print) | LCC HD2741 (ebook) | DDC
658.4—dc23/eng/20220324
LC record available at https://lccn.loc.gov/2022014410
LC ebook record available at https://lccn.loc.gov/2022014411

ISBN: 978-0-367-26694-3 (hbk)
ISBN: 978-1-032-34558-1 (pbk)
ISBN: 978-0-429-29464-8 (ebk)

DOI: 10.4324/9780429294648

Typeset in Times New Roman
by codeMantra

Contents

Illustrations

Figures

Tables

1 Introduction to Corporate Governance

The Relevance of Corporate Governance

Corporate governance has wide implications and is critical to economic and social wellbeing, firstly in providing the incentives and performance measures to achieve business success, and secondly in providing the accountability and transparency to ensure the equitable distribution of the resulting wealth. The significance of corporate governance for the stability and equity of society is captured in the definition of the concept offered by Cadbury (2000, 2002) and adopted by the World Bank:

> Corporate governance is concerned with holding the balance between economic and social goals and between individual and communal goals. The governance framework is there to encourage the efficient use of resources and equally to require accountability for the stewardship of those resources. The aim is to align as nearly as possible the interests of individuals, corporations and society.

The G20/OECD (2015) have endorsed the central importance of corporate governance for the maintenance of economic stability and the performance of corporations: "The purpose of corporate governance is to help build an environment of trust, transparency and accountability necessary for fostering long-term investment, financial stability and business integrity, thereby supporting stronger growth and more inclusive societies." Principles of corporate governance are not an end in themselves, but a framework on which to "develop more detailed mandatory or voluntary provisions that can take into account country-specific economic, legal and cultural differences."

Corporate governance essentially has three elements defining corporate purpose, balancing interests, and measuring performance.

DOI: 10.4324/9780429294648-1

Historically these elements have been broadly interpreted with a corporate *purpose* related to the wide interests of stakeholders and the community amounting to a *licence to operate*. The governance mechanisms have been understood as providing a sense of accountability, responsibility, and fairness regarding the interests of the different participants in the company. Finally, performance measurement has also been widely conceived as contributing value in financial, social, and environmental terms (Clarke 2023).

This careful historical calibration of interests was deliberately overturned by the doctrine of shareholder value and imposition of the idea of *shareholder primacy*. We are now entering an era in which the irresponsibility of such narrow estimations of corporate purpose, governance, and performance is becoming manifest. The onset of significant, damaging, and apparently relentless human- and industry-induced climate change has demanded a reconceptualisation of the business *license to operate* around the principles of sustainability (Rasche and Waddock 2014; Klein 2015).

In the past, corporate objectives described as "wealth generating" too frequently have resulted in the loss of wellbeing to communities and the ecology. But increasingly in the future, the *license to operate* will not be given so readily to corporations and other entities. A licence to operate will depend on maintaining the highest standards of integrity and practice in corporate behaviour. Corporate governance essentially will involve a sustained and responsible monitoring of not just the financial health of the company but also the social and environmental impact of the company.

In this work, the comparison and synthesis of the institutional diversity of corporate governance internationally will be placed in the context of an increasingly resource-constrained environment in which corporations will face new responsibilities and constraints. The re-evaluation of fiduciary duty is presently taking place, and will prove to be profound, as Watchman states, "The concept of fiduciary duty is organic, not static. It will continue to evolve as society changes, not least in response to the urgent need for us to move towards and environmentally, economically and socially sustainable financial system" (UNEP 2015: 9). The fundamental purpose of corporate governance will increasingly become the delivery of corporate social responsibility and sustainability (Clarke 2015, 2016; Clarke et al. 2023).

Origins of Corporate Governance

The business corporation emerged as the dominant form for business association in the early twentieth century, but its antecedents lie

800 years earlier in the notion of the corporate entity developed to resolve problems of group relations in religious and social communities. These medieval elements were transformed by the application of corporate ideas and practices of the business enterprises that came later (Redmond 2005: 28). Among these devices was the idea of the *incorporate person* – the interpretation of companies as legal persons with rights and duties. Corporate bodies recognised by common law were applied to business organisations in England and Holland when charters were granted to incorporate trading companies which became joint-stock companies. Speculative excesses quickly followed the formation of the early trading companies.

However, the principle of people managing companies being responsible for the investments of others was now well established in business organisations. The resulting concerns regarding corporate governance are not a new thing, and Adam Smith in 1776 in *The Wealth of Nations* made a comment on company management that would echo through the ages:

> Being managers of other people's money than their own, it cannot well be expected that they should watch over it with the same anxious vigilance with which the partners in a private co-partner frequently watch over their own ... Negligence and profusion, therefore, must always prevail more or less in the management of the affairs of a joint stock company.
>
> (Smith 1976: 264–265)

As technological change advanced with the industrial revolution and corporations increased in scale and activity, there occurred a wider diffusion of ownership of many large companies as no individual, family, or group of managers could provide sufficient capital to sustain growth. Berle and Means chronicled the profound implications of this *separation of ownership and control*: "the dissolution of the old atom of ownership into its component parts, control and beneficial ownership" (1933: 8). For Berle and Means, it was axiomatic that as the number of shareholders increased, their influence upon corporate enterprise diminished as professional managers took control. As corporations became the dominant vehicles of the US economy, their legal instruments of incorporation – particularly in the state of Delaware which became the most popular jurisdiction in which to incorporate – increasingly reflected the interests not of stockholders, but of the executive management who intended to run the corporation.

Berle and Means identify two distinct functions of the corporate entity, first the commercial operations, and second the business of raising capital and distributing risks, losses, and gains. Whilst managers may reasonably insist on as free a hand as possible in running commercial business activities, it is quite a different thing to allow management power to determine how the financial surplus of the corporation is distributed.

The separation of ownership and control occurs as the ownership of corporations is progressively diluted from complete ownership to minority control, and though there are many devices for working control of a corporation to be retained by those with only a minority of the shares, eventually the situation is reached when ownership is so widely distributed that no minority interest is large enough to dominate the affairs of the company. At this point, even the largest single interest amounts to just a small percentage of the total shareholdings, insufficient to place irresistible pressure upon management. Means (1931) recognises a range of potential forms of dilution of ownership control:

- control through almost complete ownership
- majority control
- control through a legal device without majority ownership
- minority control
- management control

Different mechanisms are outlined by Means by which managers are able to shift the enterprise profits, and to a considerable degree the underlying assets, among groups of stockholders (including themselves). There are countervailing forces including the need to maintain a reputation for probity if new sources of funds are to be accessed, the influence of the law and state regulation, and the intervention of the financial community. However, vigilance is required to prevent managers from acquiring absolute power.

In what became the most influential work on corporate governance in the twentieth century *The Modern Corporation and Private Property* (1933), Berle and Means anticipate the emergence of a new form of social organisation, citing Walther Rathenau who commented on similar developments in German corporate life: "The depersonalisation of ownership, the objectification of enterprise, the detachment of property from the possessor, leads to a point where the enterprise becomes transformed into an institution" (1933: 304). Berle and Means (1933: 306) acknowledge that potentially there are three forms that might emerge to govern this new corporation:

- The first is without regard for the change of character from *active* ownership to *passive* property ownership, to maintain the doctrine of strict property rights, by which the management are placed in a position of trusteeship for the *sole* benefit of the shareholders, despite the fact that the latter have ceased to have power or accept responsibility for the *active* property in which they have an interest.

- In direct opposition to the doctrine of strict property rights is the view that corporate developments have created a new set of relationships, giving to the management powers which are absolute and not limited by any implied obligation with respect to their use. This would reflect a significant modification of the principle of private property.

- A third possibility exists, however, that passive property rights should yield before the larger interests of society. The management of corporations should develop into a neutral technocracy, balancing the claims of various groups, employees, customers, shareholders, and the community, and assigning to each according to a transparent policy.

In the most passionate argument in favour of the merits of the third alternative as the right course for the future development of corporate governance, Berle and Means declare:

> Eliminating the sole interest of the passive owner, however, does not necessarily lay a basis for the alternative claim that the new powers should be used in the interest of the controlling groups. The latter have not presented, in acts or words any acceptable defence of the proposition that these powers should be so used. No tradition supports this proposition. The control groups have, rather, cleared the way for the claims of a group far wider than either the owners or the control. They have placed the community in a position to demand that the modern corporation serve not alone the owners or the control but all society. This third alternative offers a wholly new concept of corporate activity. Neither the claims of ownership nor those of control can stand against the paramount interests of the community ... It only remains for the claims of the community to be put forward with clarity and force.
>
> (1933: 309)

Almost a century after Berle and Means expressed these hopes for a different concept of the corporation with much wider accountability to the community, the issue remains one of the most alive and highly contentious dilemmas for corporate governance. The call of Berle and

Means for an increase in the recognition and scope of fiduciary duties of those who controlled corporations continues to influence legal thinking in the context of climate change and the call for more socially and environmentally responsible corporations.

Governance and Performance

Good governance has always been intuitively associated not just with soundly run but with commercially successful companies as well. Countries known for their robust governance institutions attract investment capital. This was central to the understanding of corporate governance that informed the work of the Cadbury Committee which insisted on the first page of its pioneering report:

> The country's economy depends on the drive and efficiency of its companies. Thus the effectiveness with which boards discharge their responsibilities determines Britain's competitive position. They must be free to drive their companies forward, but exercise that freedom within a framework of effective accountability. This is the essence of any system of good corporate governance.
>
> (1992: 1.1)

There is an increasing realisation that the higher standards of corporate governance are necessary not only to ensure accountability but also to positively improve corporate performance. Though the evidence relating governance reforms to performance improvement in the past has proved mixed, more sophisticated methodologies are now being applied with more promising results, with "an increasing body of finance literature suggesting companies with superior governance offer better relative investment performance or lower investment risk" (Goldman Sachs 2006: 4).

As institutional investors increasingly become the majority shareholders in listed corporations across the world, their interest in pursuing the link between governance and performance has heightened considerably. However, the question of what constitutes *value* and how it may be measured continues to be the subject of much controversy. Once company value creation could be measured solely in financial terms: it was simply a question of the company generating a profit. In this narrow view, any social costs or environmental impact of business activity could be written off as *externalities* for communities or government to deal with. This constricted set of values is now unacceptable and encounters direct challenge wherever it is still asserted. There is a strong sense emerging among both the general public and invest-ment community that the wealth-generating activities of corporations do need to be recognised and enhanced within a wider framework of social and environmental responsibility, moving "sustainability issues from the periphery of corporate strategy to the heart of it" (UNEP 2014a: 5).

Corporate Governance and Sustainability

The definition and appreciation of what constitutes wealth creation is changing in radical ways which corporations and their governance are only just beginning to contemplate (Benn and Dunphy 2006). In the past, it was all too easy for corporations to simply externalise their social and environmental costs. However, the realisation that social cohesion and ecological integrity represent values as material and val-uable as any monetary values, suggests the next great challenge for companies is to bridge the divide between corporate governance and corporate social and environmental responsibility. Corporations in-creasingly will be held to account for their social and environmental impact. In social terms, they will need to demonstrate a commitment to their employees, community, and wider society that ensures they do no harm to the health and wellbeing of people and do everything they can to improve the quality of life. In environmental terms, corpora-tions will be made to bear the cost of any impact on the environment, and there will be incentive structures to enable better responses and solutions to environmental problems. This widening of the responsi-bilities of companies will demand a new conception of corporate gov-ernance and business objectives, a new understanding of the corporate mission (UNEP 2014a, 2014b; UNEP/CISL 2014).

There is some doubt as to whether existing explanations of corpo-rate existence, activities, and objectives are adequate for the task of examining or explaining this new corporate horizon. A great deal of legal and academic thinking on corporate governance and corporate purpose remains trapped within the tight parameters of *agency the-ory*, assuming that the only real issue is *principal-agent* relations, and that delivering *shareholder value* will resolve all problems. The under-standing of the responsibilities and objectives of corporate govern-ance needs to be developed to encompass wider concerns and deeper relationships. The corporate licence to operate needs to be negoti-ated not only with shareholders but also with a much wider constitu-ency of stakeholders representing social and environmental interests. The dominant theoretical perspective in corporate governance has neglected this wider understanding of the purpose of the corporation and substituted instead a conceptually narrow view. To understand the comparative development of corporate governance, it is useful to consider the theoretical explanations that have sought to explain this phenomenon.

Agency Theory

We understand the world through evolving theoretical frameworks, and these theories inform our actions. The dominant theoretical framework for understanding corporate governance is undoubtedly agency theory, whatever its evident limitations. Rampant executives running out of control at the shareholders expense is a sharp reminder of the significant and enduring agency dilemmas in corporate governance. Agency theory conceives of the firm as a *nexus of constantly re-negotiated contracts* by individuals each aiming to maximise their own utility (Alchian and Demsetz 1972). Jensen and Meckling (1976) suggest the essence of the agency problem is the separation of finance and management. Investors (principals) need the managers' (agents) specialised human capital to generate returns on their funds.

The principals and agents effectively have an unwritten contract that specifies what managers can do with the funds, and how the returns will be divided between them and the shareholders. A problem is that as future contingencies cannot be anticipated, complete contracts are not feasible. The principals and agents have to allocate *residual control rights*: the rights to make decisions not foreseen in the contract. Managers inevitably acquire considerable residual control rights, providing discretion over how to allocate investors' funds. From this point of view, the subject of corporate governance concerns the constraints principals can put on agents to reduce the misallocation of investors' funds.

Agency theory claims shareholders have the right to residual claims since they are the residual risk bearers: the only economic actors who make an investment in the corporation without a contractual guarantee of a specific return. As the *residual claimants*, shareholders bear the risk of the company making a profit or a loss, and they have a direct interest in the allocation of corporate resources to make the largest residual possible. As the basis of agency theory is the *self-interested utility-maximising motivation* of individual actors, it is assumed the relationship between shareholders and managers will be problematic, and there is a single-minded focus on how the principal is able to prevent the agent from maximising his own utility (Jensen 1994).

For agency theorists, efficient *markets in corporate control*, management, and information are the means that militate against the agency problem. However, as *agency dilemmas* are so inherent in the corporate form, the universality of the publicly listed corporation is a phenomenon of enduring concern:

> Why, given the existence of positive costs of the agency relationship, do we find the usual corporate form of organisation with widely diffuse ownership so widely prevalent. If one takes seriously much of the literature regarding the "discretionary" power held by management of large corporations, it is difficult to understand the historical fact of enormous growth in equity in such organisations not only in the United States, but throughout the world.
>
> (Jensen and Meckling 1976: 330)

The way agency theory has come to dominate so completely the corporate governance literature is explained by Daily et al. (2003: 372) as due to two factors:

> First, it is an extremely simple theory, in which large corporations are reduced to two participants – managers and shareholders – and the interests of each are assumed to be both clear and consistent. Second, the notion of humans as self-interested and generally unwilling to sacrifice personal interests for the interests of others is both age old and widespread ... Economists struggled with this problem for centuries until Jensen and Meckling (1976) provided their convincing rationale for how the public corporation could survive and prosper despite the self-interested proclivities of managers. In nearly all modern governance research governance mechanisms are conceptualised as deterrents to managerial self-interest.

Double Agency Dilemmas

Agency theory does address some of the central dilemmas associated with the transformation of the simple control structures of the owner entrepreneur company, to the more complex controls required following the separation of ownership and control. However, agency theory underestimates and over-simplifies the complexity of many corporate relationships and purposes and distils these down to the simple mechanisms of principal/agent tensions. There is to begin with what is in effect a *double agency dilemma*, firstly in the relationship between shareholders and board of directors, and secondly in the relationship between board of directors and management. Yet agency theory concentrates all its attention on the shareholders/directors dilemma, and scarcely ever enters the "black box" of the firm to consider the relationship between boards of directors and management. Despite this constricted focus, it is the fundamental tenets of agency theory that have informed much of corporate governance policy and practice in recent decades:

> The dominant view of boards, a view that had underpinned the majority of reform activity, is that the board acts as a control mechanism to reduce the potential divergence of interests between corporate management and shareholders. Non-executive directors, because of their supposed independence and objectivity, provide an important check and balance to the power of the chief executive and his or her executive team. The notion of "contestability" in the boardroom has become central, and the model for boards is unmistakably adversarial.
>
> (Stiles and Taylor 2002: 1)

The translation of the complexities of the corporate world into a simple set of control relationships neglects the political, organisational, and technical dimensions of business activity that make it less predictable and controllable than it might appear:

> Agency theorists need to assume not only that people are self-seeking economic utility maximisers, but that they are fully competent self-seeking utility maximisers. In other words, they need to assume that, faced with particular choices, people will in fact make the decisions that maximise their utility ... Nobody with any knowledge of business would suggest that all managers are equally competent or that any manager can infallibly achieve their objectives, whether these are the objectives set by their shareholders or those dictated by their own self-interest. The world of business is simply not like that. On the contrary, it is confused, uncertain and unpredictable. The information on which decisions have to be based is both insufficient and overwhelming and can be full of contradictions. Implementation of a decision can be wrecked by a host of technical, personal and interpersonal factors quite outside a chief executive's control. The most carefully and competently constructed judgements, whether they be executive judgements of how to run the business, or non-executive judgements of how

the executives are performing, can with hindsight appear fatally flawed.

(Hendy 2005: 58)

This is not to suggest that the effort to exercise effective control and coherent direction in corporate enterprise is futile, but it does imply that the application of simple rules or the assumption of crude inter- pretations of motivation is likely to be inappropriate. The effort to understand and to bring into some alignment the interests of share- holders, the activities and aspirations of managers, and the concerns of wider stakeholders requires more careful analysis and application than agency theory might offer. As Pye and Pettigrew (2005: 30) argue:

> The idea that all managers are self-interested agents who do not bear the full financial effects of their decisions (Jensen and Meck- ling 1976) has provided an extraordinary edifice around which three decades of agency research has been built, even though these assumptions are simplistic and lead to a reductionist view of busi- ness, that is, comprising two participants – managers (agents) and shareholders (principals).

Attempting a deeper understanding of corporate governance relation- ships requires consideration of wider theoretical perspectives.

More Complex Theories of Corporate Governance

For too long, corporate governance has been observed through a single analytical lens of agency theory that offers partial insights but cannot begin to examine the full dimensions of the problem or offer convincing explanations. The complexity and richness of the dynamic phenomena involved in corporate governance requires the application of a range of theoretical critiques to understand more fully the dilemmas involved:

> A multi-theoretic approach to corporate governance is essential for recognising the many mechanisms and structures that might reasonably enhance organisational functioning. For example, the board of directors is perhaps the most central internal governance mechanism. Whereas agency theory is appropriate for conceptual- ising the control/monitoring role of directors, additional (and per- haps contrasting) theoretical perspectives are needed to explain director's resource, service and strategy roles.

(Daily et al. 2003: 372)

Existing theoretical approaches to corporate governance follow a continuum from the narrow focus of agency theory and transaction cost theory inspired by financial economics, through approaches including stewardship, resource dependency, stakeholder and managerialist theories developed by organisational theorists, to more critical analysis originating in sociological and political critiques (Clarke 2004). Each theoretical approach has its own logic and limitations, and though a number of the approaches represent opposing interpretations of the same problem, in some cases, the theories serve to illuminate different dimensions of the governance problem.

After agency theory, the most established theoretical approach is transaction cost economics. Ronald Coase (1937) insisted, notwithstanding the assumption of neoclassical theory that the allocation of resources is coordinated through a series of exchange transactions on the market, that in the real world a considerable proportion of economic activity is organised in firms. Coase examines the economic explanation for the existence of firms, and why economic activities take place within firms rather than through markets. He explains the nature of firms in terms of the imperfections of markets, and in terms of the *transaction costs* of market exchange.

New institutional economics differs from agency theory in that the corporate governance problems of firms are perceived to proceed from a number of contractual hazards. This approach is concerned with discovering internal measures and mechanisms which reduce costs associated with contractual hazards to an efficient level: the external discipline of the market cannot be relied on to mitigate these problems, as it has only "limited constitutional powers to conduct audits and has limited access to the firm's incentive and resource allocation machinery" (Williamson 1979: 143). Like neo-classical economics though, the locus of attention remains the shareholder-manager relationship, but in this case, it is because shareholders are perceived to "face a diffuse but significant risk of expropriation because the assets in question are numerous and ill-defined, and cannot be protected in a well-focused, transaction specific way" (Williamson 1985: 1210; Learmount 2002: 5). As with agency theory, the narrowness of the focus limits the explanatory power of this analysis.

Relationship and Resource-Based Theories of Governance

In contrast to agency theory, stewardship theory acknowledges a larger range of human motives of managers, including orientations towards achievement, altruism, and the commitment to meaningful work.

Stewardship theory maintains there is no inherent conflict of interest between managers and owners, and that optimum governance structures allow coordination of the enterprise to be achieved most effectively. Managers should be authorised to act since according to stewardship theory, they are not opportunistic agents but good *stewards* who will act in the best interests of owners. Stewardship theory recognises a strong relationship between managers' pursuit of the objectives of the enterprise, the owners' satisfaction, and other participants in the enterprise reward. Davis et al. (1997) suggest that as managers maximise shareholders' wealth through raising the performance of the firm, they serve their own purposes. Managers balance competing shareholder and stakeholder objectives, making decisions in the best interests of all. However, there is an element of choice in corporate governance arrangements – both managers and owners can choose to have either agency or steward relationships, contingent upon their assessment of the motivations of each other, and the situation of the enterprise. Stewardship theory rescues the integrity of management as a profession, something many managers would recognise and aspire towards.

There is a stream of theoretical approaches that widen the focus beyond internal monitoring, to explore the external challenges of corporate governance in terms of building relationships and securing resources. Resource dependence theory, institutional theory, and network theory all are interested in the external relations of corporations. Resource dependency theory highlights the *interdependencies* of organisations rather than viewing them simply in terms of management intentions. Hillman et al. (2000), for example, examine how company directors may serve to connect the firm with external resources that help to overcome uncertainty, and provide access to relationships with suppliers, buyers, public policy makers, and other social groups. Resource dependency approaches add a vital external dimension to corporate governance relationships.

Stakeholder theory defines organisations as *multilateral* agreements between the enterprise and its multiple stakeholders. The relationship between the company and its *internal stakeholders* (employees, managers, and owners) is framed by formal and informal rules developed through the history of the relationship. This institutional setting constrains and creates the strategic possibilities for the company. While management may receive finance from shareholders, they depend upon employees to fulfil the productive purpose and strategic intentions of the company. *External stakeholders* (customers, suppliers, competitors, special interest groups, and the community) are equally important and are constrained also by formal and informal rules that businesses must respect. Stakeholder theory has an intellectual appeal and practical application; however, it is argued often that multiple stakeholder responsibilities can leave management with too much freedom of manoeuvre (often by managers who do not wish to be more widely accountable!).

Critical Perspectives

From a more critical perspective, managerialist theory focuses on the distinctions between the myth and the reality of the relative powers of managers and boards. Mace (1971), for example, examines the 1960s ascendancy of corporate executives, when powerful chief executive officers (CEOs) selected and controlled the boards of directors of the companies they ran. He outlines how CEOs in the US were able to determine board membership, to decide what boards could and could not do, controlled the information and professional advice the board received, and determined the compensation of senior executives, including often themselves. When corporations fail, the question always arises: *Where were the board of directors?* However, there is a wide gap between what directors are supposed to do, what people generally assume directors do, and what they are actually allowed to do in practice.

Mace catalogues how dysfunctional boards rather than being exceptional became normal in the US, as executives took control. Finally, there are more radical theoretical critiques which suggest that corporations perpetuate the power of an elite, serving to exploit others in the interests of accumulating wealth and power (Mills 1971). Though radical analysis faded after the 1960s, it has enjoyed a new lease of life in the widespread critique of the impact of globalisation which corporations have spearheaded, and in the critique of the sustainability of corporations (Fleming and Spicer 2007; Weinstein 2012, 2013; Baars and Spicer 2017; Clarke et al. 2019).

Complementary Theories of Corporate Governance

Adopting and synthesising different theoretical perspectives may begin to provide a fuller understanding of the mechanisms and processes of corporate governance. In a survey of board practice, Philip Stiles and Bernard Taylor recommend the explanatory power of a series of theoretical perspectives. The structure of the board, its monitoring of budgets and plans, and its address to performance and targets, all reflect the assumptions of agency theory and transaction cost theory underpinning the control role of the board:

Consistent with this theme, however, is the finding that boards may actively help companies to unlearn organisational practices that have become dysfunctional (Nystrom and Starbuck 1984). That is, boards may diagnose new opportunities, select new performance measures, and emphasise certain control systems at the expense of others, in order to bring the organisation to a new focus. This supports the stewardship theory of board activity and suggests that, in certain circumstances, both organisational economics and stewardship theories may be complementary. The combination of what Tricker (1994) calls the conformance and performance roles suggests that multiple theoretical lenses are appropriate. Reinforcing the case for complementary theoretical perspectives is the evidence of boundary-spanning activity on the part of non-executive directors but also of the executive directors, providing support for the resource-dependence view of board activity. Our approach is, therefore, in line with greater calls for reconciliation between economic and organisational perspectives (Kosnik 1987; Eisenhardt 1989; Judge and Zeithaml 1992) and shows that seemingly contradictory approaches can coexist as theoretical explanations.

(Stiles and Taylor 2002: 122–123)

There are many other established and emerging theoretical tools that may enhance the understanding of corporate governance, however, and they may prove increasingly necessary, given the decisive challenges ahead. The essential and eternal concept of *trust* is a good place to commence. Trust is a vital component of corporate governance, and the absence of trust is deeply corrosive. As Stiles and Taylor (2002: 23) note, much of the activity of corporate governance revolves around the building of trust:

A series of studies by Westphal and Zajac has highlighted how the interpersonal influence processes in the board/chief executive relationship can help trust and cooperation develop within the board and help problem-solving and decision-making activity (Westphal and Zajac 1995, 1997; Zajac and Westphal 1996).

In their research on boards, Stiles and Taylor (2002: 123–124) indicate how trust and control are not mutually exclusive:

Underpinning the discussion has been the central role of trust in enhancing both board task performance and board cohesiveness. The model of trust argued for has not been the traditional one of trust and control conceptualised as opposite ends of a continuum. Rather trust and control are interdependent. Because the board operates in complex and uncertain conditions and is often characterised by role conflict the potential for both trust and control to coexist is apparent. Control mechanisms serve to focus members' attention on organisational goals, while trust mechanisms promote decision-making and enhance cohesiveness.

Team Production Theory

Another tributary of ideas has offered a more thoughtful interpretation of the corporate governance dilemma. *Team production* theory, initiated by Alchian and Demsetz, comprehends something of the collaborative basis of business endeavour that was fundamental to earlier theorists. The reformulation of team production theory by Margaret Blair and Lynn Stout presents a recognisable and meaningful explanation of the purpose of the corporation and the duties of directors. Rather than conceiving of the company as a bundle of assets that belong to shareholders, Blair (1995) argues corporations may be conceived as institutional arrangements for governing the relationships between all of the parties that contribute firm-specific assets. This includes not only shareholders, but also long-term employees who develop specialised skills of value to the corporation, and suppliers, customers, and others who make specialised investments.

If the job of management is to maximise the total wealth of the enterprise rather than just the value of the shareholders' stake, then management must take into account the effect of corporate decisions on all stakeholders in the firm. In adapting the *nexus of contracts* theory, Blair and Stout (1999, 2001; Kaufman and Englander 2005) consider shareholders as only one of the parties that make a contribution to the firm, and effectively are not the only residual claimants of the firm. Other groups, including employees, creditors, managers, and government, make contributions to ensure the enterprise will succeed. The assets created are generally firm-specific and, once committed to team production, cannot be withdrawn and sold elsewhere for their full value. Blair and Stout provide an expansive adaption of the original theoretical framework of Alchian and Demsetz (who themselves did not use the concept of "nexus of contract," though it is closely associated with their work).

For Blair and Stout, team production theory with the board of directors serving as a *mediating hierarchy* between the different interests provides a sound foundation for conceiving of the corporation in both law and practice:

We believe, however, that our mediating hierarchy approach, which views public corporation law as a mechanism for filling in the gaps where team members have found explicit contracting difficult or impossible, is consistent with the "nexus of contracts" approach to understanding corporate law. The "nexus of contracts" view of the firm holds that relationships in the firm should be understood as an intertwined set of relationships between parties who agree to work with each other in pursuit of mutual benefit, even though not all the relationships that comprise a firm are necessarily spelled out in complete "contracts." It might perhaps be more informative to think of corporations, and hierarchical governance structures within corporations, as institutional substitutes for contracts, just as property rights are an institutional substitute and necessary precondition for contracts. Nevertheless, we locate the mediating hierarchy model of the public corporation within the nexus of contracts tradition because in the model, team members voluntarily choose to submit themselves to the hierarchy as an efficient arrangement that furthers their own self-interests.

(Blair and Stout 1999: 254)

Deakin advances further the idea of the corporation as an essentially collaborative institution. He argues the concept of the corporation as a *commons* or shared societal resource is more consistent with its legal nature and offers the possibility of realigning corporate governance (Deakin et al. 2017):

To describe the corporation as an *institutional commons* in the sense identified by Elinor Ostrom (Ostrom, 1990; Poteete, Janssen and Ostrom, 2011) is not to claim that it is completely ownerless. The commons as a whole cannot be owned, but there are numerous property-type claims in and over the resources contained within it. These are not simply the shareholders' rights of exclusion and alienation identified by corporate law scholarship, but rights of access, withdrawal and management which frequently vest in other stakeholder groups, including employees and creditors, but also fiscal and regulatory bodies. The task of governing the corporation is the same as that of governing all other commons, which is to devise a set of norms which will enable the overlapping and competing claims of the different stakeholder groups to be reconciled, with a view to sustaining the common resource on which they all, in different ways, depend. Company law, as an evolved response to the coordination problems inherent in the business enterprise, very well exemplifies Ostrom's focus on institutional evolution as the basis for effective and sustainable governance arrangements.

(Deakin et al. 2017)

Whilst such radical reconceptualisation of the corporation are rare, it is likely that to meet the imminent challenge of social and environmental sustainability in a post-carbon economy, further profound rethinking of corporate form, purpose, governance, and directors' duties will be an essential and very practical task.

Other theoretical perspectives may well contribute to a radical reconceptualisation of corporate governance around theories such as *social capital* that conceives of value creation arising in social relationships; the *knowledge-based theory of the firm* which acknowledges the increasing importance of intellectual capital as the basis of value creation in the knowledge economy; theories that see the firm as a *complex adaptive system* that wrestles with and adapts to its competitive economic environment; theories of *creativity and innovation*; and most important of all the theory of *sustainability*, and whether the corporation can become a sustainable form of economic activity. These approaches all demand that corporate governance can only be understood by going beyond the shareholder/manager relationship, and the immediate mechanisms and institutions of governance, to a deeper understanding of the relationships between corporations and the economies and societies they serve (Clarke 2004).

References

Alchian, A. and Demsetz, H. (1972) Production, Information Costs, and Economic Organisation, *American Economic Review*, 62: 777–795.

Baars, G. and Spicer, A. (2017) *The Corporation*, Cambridge: Cambridge University Press.

Benn, S. and Dunphy, D. C. (2006) *Corporate Governance and Sustainability: Challenges for Theory and Practice*. London, New York: Routledge.

Berle, A.A. and Means, G.C. (1933) *The Modern Corporation and Private Property*, Riverwoods, IL: Commerce Clearing House.

Blair, M.M. (1995) *Ownership and Control: Rethinking Corporate Governance for the 21st Century*, Washington, DC: Brookings Institute.

Blair, M.M. and Stout, L.A. (1999) A Team Production Theory of Corporate Law, *Virginia Law Review*, 85(2): 247–328.

Blair, M.M. and Stout, L.A. (2001) Director Accountability and the Mediating Role of the Corporate Board, *Washington University Law Quarterly*, 79: 403.

Cadbury, A. (1992) *Report of the Committee on the Financial Aspects of Corporate Governance*, London: Gee & Co.

Cadbury, A. (2000) *World Bank, Corporate Governance: A Framework for Implementation* (Foreword), Washington, DC: World Bank.

Cadbury, A. (2002) *Corporate Governance and Chairmanship*, Oxford: Oxford University Press.

Clarke, T. (2004) Cycles of Crisis and Regulation: The Enduring Agency and Stewardship Problems of Corporate Governance, *Corporate Governance: An International Review*, 12(2): 153–161.

Clarke, T. (2015) The Long Road to Reformulating the Understanding of Directors' Duties: Legalizing Team Production Theory? *Seattle University Law Review*, 38: 437–490.

Clarke, T. (2016) The Widening Scope of Directors Duties: The Increasing Impact of Corporate Social and Environmental Responsibility, *Seattle University Law Review*, 39: 531–578.

Clarke, T. (2023) *International Corporate Governance*, London and New York: Routledge, 2007; Third Edition.

Clarke, T., Edwards, M. and Benn, S. (2023) *The Routledge Companion to Corporate Sustainability*, London: Routledge.

Clarke, T., O'Brien, J. and O'Kelley, C. (2019) *The Oxford Handbook of the Corporation*, Oxford: Oxford University Press.

Coase, R. (1937) The Nature of the Firm, *Economica*, 4: 386–405.

Daily, C.M., Dalton, D.R. and Cannella, A.C. (2003) Corporate Governance: Decades of Dialogue and Data, *Academy of Management Review*, 28(3): 371–382.

Davis, J.H., Schoorman, F.D. and Donaldson, L. (1997) Toward a Stewardship Theory of Management, *The Academy of Management Review*, 22(1): 20–47.

Deakin, S., Gindis, D., Hodgson, G., Kainan, H. and Pistor, K. (2017) Legal Institutionalism: Capitalism and the Constitutive Role of Law, *Journal of Comparative Economics*, 45: 1.

Fleming, P. and Spicer, A. (2007) *Contesting the Corporation Struggle, Power and Resistance in Organizations.* Cambridge: Cambridge University Press.

G20/OECD (2015) *Principles of Corporate Governance*, Paris: OECD Publishing.

Goldman Sachs JB Were (2006) *Good Corporate Governance=Good Investment Returns*, Melbourne: Goldman Sachs JB Were.

Hendy, J. (2005) Beyond Self-Interest: Agency Theory and the Board in a Satisficing World, *British Journal of Management*, 16: S55–S63.

Hillman, A.J., Cannella, A.A. and Paetzold, R.L. (2000) The Resource Dependence Role of Corporate Directors: Strategic Adaptation of Board Composition in Response to Environmental Change, *Journal of Management Studies*, 37: 235–254.

Jensen, M.C. (1994) Self-interest, Altruism, Incentives and Agency Theory, *Journal of Applied Corporate Finance*, Summer: 7(2): 40–55.

Jensen, M.C. and Meckling, W.H. (1976) Theory of the Firm, Managerial Behaviour, Agency Costs and Ownership Structure, *Journal of Financial Economics*, 3(4) October: 305–360.

Kaufman, D. and Englander, E.J. (2005) A Team Production Model of Corporate Governance, *Academy of Management Executive*, 19(3): 9–22.

Klein, N. (2015) *This Changes Everything: Capitalism versus the Climate*, London: Penguin.

Learmont, S. (2002) *Corporate Governance: What Can Be Learned from Japan?* Oxford: Oxford University Press.

Mace (1971) *Directors: Myth and Reality*, Boston, MA: Harvard University Press.

Means, G.C. (1931; 2005) The Separation of Ownership and Control in American Industry, *Quarterly Journal of Economics*, 46(1): 68–100, in T. Clarke, *Corporate Governance: Critical Perspectives in Business and Management*, vol. I. *The Genesis of Corporate Governance*, London: Routledge, 2005.

Mills, C. Wright (1971) *The Power Elite*, New York: Oxford University Press.

Ostrom, E. (1990) *Governing the Commons: The Evolution of Institutions for Collective Action*, Cambridge: Cambridge University Press.

Poteete, A., Janssen, M. and Ostrom, E. (2011) *Working Together: Collective Action, the Commons, and Multiple Methods in Practice*, Princeton, NJ: Princeton University Press.

Pye, A. and Pettigrew, A. (2005) Studying Board Context, Process and Dynamics: Some Challenges for the Future, *British Journal of Management*, 16: S27–S38.

Rasche, A. and Waddock, S. (2014) Global Sustainability Governance and the UN Global Compact, *Journal of Business Ethics*, 122(2): June III, 209–216.

Redmond, P. (2005) *Companies and Securities Law: Commentary and Materials*, Thomson Lawbook, Sydney: LBC.

Smith, A. (1976) *An Inquiry into the Nature and Causes of the Wealth of Nations* (1776), Chicago, IL: University of Chicago Press.

Stiles, P. and Taylor, B. (2002) *Boards at Work: How Directors View Their Roles and Responsibilities*, Oxford: Oxford University Press.

UNEP (2014a) *Integrated Governance: A New Model of Governance for Sustainability*, Geneva: UNEP Financial Initiative Asset Management Working Group.

UNEP (2014b) *Financial Institutions Taking Action on Climate Change*, Geneva: UNEP Financial Initiative Asset Management Working Group, UNEP.

UNEP (2015) *Fiduciary Duty in the 21st Century*, United Nations Environment Program http://www.unepfi.org/fileadmin/documents/fiduciary_duty_21st_century.pdf.

UNEP/CISL (2014) *Stability and Sustainability in Banking Reform*, Cambridge: UNEP Financial Initiative/ University of Cambridge/Institute for Sustainability Leadership (CISL).

Weinstein, O. (2012) Firm, Property and Governance: From Berle and Means to the Agency Theory, and beyond, *Accounting, Economics and Law: A Convivium*, 2(2): 43–60.

Weinstein, O. (2013) The Shareholder Model of the Corporation, Between Mythology and Reality, *Accounting, Economics and Law: A Convivium*, 3(1): 1–55.

Westphal, J.D. and Zajac, E.J. (1995) Defections from the Inner Circle: Social Exchange, Reciprocity and the Diffusion of Board Independence in US Corporations, *Academy of Management Best Papers Proceedings*, 281–285.

Westphal, J.D. and Zajac, E.J. (1997) Defections from the Inner Circle: Social Exchange, Reciprocity, and the Diffusion of Board Independence in U.S. Corporations, *Administrative Science Quarterly*, 42: 161–183.

Williamson, O.E. (1979) Transaction-Cost Economics: The Governance of Contractual Relations, *Journal of Law and Economics*, 22: 233–261.

Williamson, O.E. (1985) *The Economic Institutions of Capitalism*, New York: Free Press.

Zajac, E.J. and Westphal, J.D. (1996) Director Reputation, CEO-Board Power, and the Dynamics of Board Interlocks, *Administrative Science Quarterly*, 41: 507–529.

2 International Diversity of Modes of Corporate Governance

Institutional Diversity in International Corporate Governance

Different approaches to business formation and the accompanying corporate governance structures and regulations have evolved in different social and economic contexts. Among the more important contextual and industrial variables that influence the business form and system of corporate governance adopted are:

- national, regional and cultural differences;
- ownership structure and dispersion;
- the industry and market environment of the corporation;
- firm size and structure;
- lifecycle variations, including origin and development, technology, and periodic crises and new directions;
- CEO tenure, attributes, and background (Huse 2005: 68).

In the historical evolution of corporate governance in different regional cultures and countries, different choices were made about the most efficient company structures to adopt, and the appropriate forms of regulation. At the time of first business formation, fundamental questions were posed, which by now have been largely forgotten:

> What should be the purpose of the corporation? Is it a community of human beings, a nexus of contracts, or the possession of its shareholders? Do corporations incur social obligations in return for the privileges that society grants to them? What constitutes a fair distribution of rewards from economic activity?
>
> (Jacoby 2001: 27)

DOI: 10.4324/9780429294648-2

In the study of comparative corporate governance, it is important to return to these fundamental questions in explaining the divergence and convergence of governance approaches: "Why did corporate governance systems develop differently in these different countries? Which system does a better job at solving the problems of corporate governance? Will corporations in different countries converge to a similar system of corporate governance?" (McDonnell 2002: 2).

In the rich diversity of corporate governance forms internationally, there is a clear divergence between *outsider* systems found in Anglo-American countries with dispersed equity markets, separation of ownership, and control and disclosure-based regulation, and *insider* systems which predominate in Europe, Asia-Pacific, and other regions of the world, with concentrated ownership, bank finance, and the representation of majority interests on the board of directors.

As important as the different ownership and regulatory structures adopted in the divergent governance systems are the distinctive relationships forged and objectives pursued (Table 2.1). The outsider system is oriented very strongly towards shareholders and perceives the major corporate objective as the delivery of shareholder value (often in the short term). In contrast, the insider system is built on close relationships with a wide range of stakeholders and conceives of the corporate mission as the creation of values for all stakeholders in perpetuity. With the increasing ascendancy of capital markets, the dominance of the Anglo-American approach to corporate governance over other systems is often assumed, though the strengths and weaknesses of all approaches need to be considered:

> Anglo-American finance economists are fond of touting the efficiency advantages of shareholder governance; they are convinced of the superiority of institutional arrangements in their home countries. But the fact of the matter is, each corporate governance system has attached to it a complex set of costs and benefits. Accurately toting up and comparing these sets is difficult if not impossible; claims of superiority are wishful thinking.
>
> (Jacoby 2001: 18)

For those who think there will be a ready global convergence towards a uniform Anglo-American system of corporate governance, the rich diversity of political forms of governance in the developed world is a useful reminder of the institutional diversity that has survived and is

Table 2.1 Properties of Insider and Outsider Systems of Corporate Governance

Properties	Outsider Systems (Shareholder Model)	Insider Systems (Stakeholder Model)
Ownership	Dispersed ownership (Many owners often have a transitory interest in the firm)	Concentrated ownership (The owners tend to have an enduring interest in the company)
Control	Separation of ownership and control (Little incentive for outside investors to participate in corporate control)	Association of ownership with control (Control by interested parties (banks, related firms, and employees). Owners often hold board positions. In some systems recognition of formal rights of employees)
Law	Liberal corporate law, strict security law	Strict corporate law, liberal security law
Finance	Low debt/equity ratio and low ratio of bank credits to total liabilities	High debt to equity ratio and high ratio of bank credits to total liabilities
	Highly sophisticated and diversified financial markets	Low level of sophistication and low opportunities for diversification of financial markets
Growth	Merger and acquisition (Growth through takeover of other firms)	Organic growth (Growth through generation internally of new value and opportunities)
Takeovers	Hostile takeovers that are often costly and antagonistic	Absence of hostile takeovers (Often crossholdings and understandings between firms in the same industry)
Orientation	Short-term	Long-term
Management mission	Performance of assets to release shareholder value	Stewardship of business institution to achieve long-term stakeholder values
Business strategy	Low commitment of outsider investors to long-term strategies of firms	Interested parties contribute to strategy
	While constant pressure for financial performance	Critical intervention by outside investors limited to periods of clear financial failure
	Competitive strategy, marketing, and profitability priorities	Production strategy, operations, quality, and sales volume priorities

Properties	Outsider Systems (Shareholder Model)	Insider Systems (Stakeholder Model)
Stakeholders	Interests of other stakeholders are not represented	Other stakeholders are fully recognised and sometimes represented
Weaknesses	Takeovers may create monopolies	Insider systems may encourage collusion
	Narrow focus on financial indicators can restrict strategic vision and investment	Lack of competition may inhibit radical innovation
	Managers may become self-interested	Social obligations may slow necessary restructuring

Source: Adapted from: Corbett, J. and Mayer, C. (1991), 'Financial Reform in Eastern Europe: Progress with the Wrong Model', *Oxford Review of Economic Policy*, 7, 57–75. Charkham, J. (1992), 'Corporate Governance: Lessons from Abroad', *European Business Journal*, 4(2): 8–16. Ebster-Grusz, D. and Pugh, D.S. (1992), Anglo-German Business Collaboration, *British Academy of Management Conference*, Bradford University. Nunnenkampf, P. (1996), 'The German Model of Corporate Governance: Basic Features, Critical Issues, and Applicability to Transition Economies', Working Paper, 713, Kiel Institute of World Economics; Berndt, M. (2000). "Global Differences in Corporate Governance Systems Theory and Implications for Reforms", Harvard Law School ISSN 1045-6333.

valued (and represents the different political arenas in which corporate governance legal and regulatory reform will take place).

Corporate Governance Regimes

The institutional elements of corporate governance provide the vital forces for the formation, growth, and development of corporate life in any economy. The financial and legal institutions allow the means of finance, offer guidance and monitoring, and are the source of regulation and control. The governance structures of companies are constructed around these institutions, remain closely involved in meeting their requirements, and are ultimately constrained by the surrounding institutional structures.

The role and significance of market institutions varies among governance systems. Historically, it is clear that different corporate governance regimes in different regions and countries of the world helped to provide durable advantages that were not available elsewhere. There are different equity ownership structures in the regions of the world, with institutional investors playing a dominant role in the US and the UK, and crossholding of shares in industrial groups by non-financial enterprises still prevalent in Germany and France.

Corporate governance regimes are often distinguished between the outsider systems of market-based economies such as the US and the UK, and insider systems of relationship-based economies such as practised in European or Asian countries. Each of these systems of corporate governance has inherent strengths and weaknesses as demonstrated in recent times. The outsider system of market-based corporate governance that prevails in the US and the UK character-ised by dispersed ownership and the primacy of shareholder value is the dominant force in international corporate governance. Here, the principal/agent problems are assumed to be paramount.

The market-based approach has contributed to the dynamism and growth of the US and other economies that have adopted it but expe-rienced a major reversal in the failure of Enron and a number of other large corporations, that led to the Sarbanes–Oxley Act which rein-forced the commitment to transparency and disclosure. More seriously the systemic weaknesses of the Anglo-American approach were starkly highlighted in the global financial crisis, the epicentres for which were New York and London. The financial crisis seriously damaged the economies of all of the countries that experienced it and nearly caused the collapse of the global economy.

In Europe, a relationship-based system of corporate governance has prevailed, reflecting the rich cultural diversity of the continent, and different corporate history and values. These insider systems are more dependent on loans from banks than the equity markets and tend to have the support of close business networks that have sometimes been accused of being self-serving. The European corporate govern-ance system has largely demonstrated more stability than the Anglo-American system, but this is sometimes interpreted rather as a lack of market dynamism in European economies relative to market-driven Anglo-American economies.

Finally, there are the family-based corporate structures of Asia-Pacific, again reflecting different cultural traditions and aspirations. A period of exceptionally strong economic growth ended with the East Asian financial crisis of 1997/1998, and since then, as further economic expansion has occurred, more attention has focused on strengthening the institutional foundations of corporate governance in the region.

Though there is much evidence of convergence of the regional corpo-rate governance systems around some common international principles, there remains a widespread commitment to diversity of approaches in practice. Differences in approach do reflect fundamental differences in how the values and objectives of corporations are interpreted, whether it is simply sufficient to focus on shareholder returns, or whether the firm is there to serve a much wider set of stakeholder interests? This leads to a questioning of the ultimate goals of business corporations, for example, in the light of the increasing demand worldwide for businesses to be more socially responsible and environmentally sustainable. Corporate governance involves balancing complex interests in the pursuit of value creation for the benefit of a wide constituency.

In the past, the focus of corporate governance in the Anglo-American countries was on the relationship of corporations to widely dispersed shareholders through the stock market; in the European system, the emphasis concerned the relationship of corporations with the banks and major shareholders; and in Asia, the interest was in the connection between dominant family shareholdings and corporations. There is increasing evidence emerging that a new corporate governance environment is developing in all of the regions with the dramatic increase in the scale and impact of equity markets and other financial markets, and the burgeoning growth, activity, and influence of the institutional investors.

The investment institutions have been around for a long time, but for some years, the phenomenal and sustained growth of the institutions (with the growth in wealth and pensions as economies have expanded in recent decades) has placed them at the forefront of the responsibility to ensure corporate governance is working. The total assets of the investment funds, insurance companies, and pension funds now each amount to many trillions of dollars worldwide. With the capacity to own the majority of listed company shares in all of the markets of the world, and to have a substantial presence in bond and credit markets also, the investment institutions' objectives and values will have a critical bearing on how the corporate governance system develops internationally. As the International Corporate Governance Network which represents US$54 trillion of investor funds proposes:

> As sophisticated investors with influence, often including voting rights, institutional investors have a unique leadership opportunity to encourage appropriate behaviours by their investee companies. They should play an active role as responsible investors, promoting corporate governance and other best practices at investee companies by engaging with them on pertinent financial and other relevant matters. This should help foster sustainable long-term performance by these companies to the benefit of all investors. In this

way, investment institutions will be fulfilling their core role as a fiduciary, mandated to invest in the interests of their ultimate clients or beneficiaries.

(ICGN 2013: 4)

Historical Evolution of Regional Governance Systems

The historical evolution of the regional governance systems has proved very different in orientation and outcome. Contrasting systems of corporate governance are largely built around different sources of funding and methods of monitoring. This different approach to financing and regulating corporations in the regions of the world has prevailed since the separate origins of capitalism in those places. The evolution of the corporate form can be traced from the common origin in the family and closely held capitalism of the early nineteenth century with the protection of ownership rights; through to the managerial capitalism of the early twentieth century with further protection for listed corporations and limited liability, and the refinement of the basic mechanisms of governance in the general meeting of shareholders and board of directors. Finally, the popular capitalism of the late twentieth century developed with the protection of minority interests, the reassertion of increasing board control over managers and the arrival of mass ownership in the institutional investors.

Different routes were followed in this contrasting evolution of corporate governance in the regions of the world. As a result, different destinations were reached in corporate practice, company law, and associated institutional development in Anglo-American, European, and Asian forms of corporate enterprise, and further varieties of institutions exist in the emerging economies of the world. In the Asian system of corporate governance, significant elements of family ownership survive intact, and in the European system, managerial forms have survived in a robust form. From this contrasting trajectory, two main parallel universes of corporate governance have emerged:

- *a dispersed ownership* model characterised by strong and liquid securities markets, high disclosure standards, high market transparency, and where the market for corporate control is the ultimate disciplining mechanism; and,
- *a concentrated ownership* model characterised by controlling shareholders, weak securities markets, low transparency and disclosure standards, and often a central monitoring role for large banks who have a stake in the company (Coffee 2002; Clarke

2005). Influenced by these ownership models, different institutional structures were built under the two regimes.

Types of Boards: Unitary and Supervisory Boards

Boards of directors of companies are the most critical institutional institution of corporate governance and reflect the diversity of insider and outsider systems in both the purpose assigned to boards and the structure and processes of boards. It is clear that universally boards of directors have evolved over time in response to internal dynamics, changes in the market environment, and developments in company law. In every company, the board goes through a lifecycle paralleling the life of the company from the early imperative at inception to find capital, build product markets, and establish operating principles; and later to the more considered tasks of maintaining the values and viability of the mature organisation. Boards negotiate order through their different experiences:

> In broad terms, what we have seen through the empirical data is a view of boards whose members, through a complex interplay of context, individual abilities, and structural conditions, actively negotiate over time their respective roles and the social order of the board as a whole. With the legal duties of the board underdescribing the de facto operations of board running, and regulations and codes of practice covering only part of board endeavour, ultimately the board's mandate will mean different things to different people, and negotiation is needed to achieve order in the context of change.
>
> (Hosking 1996: 342)

Although in virtually all systems, a board of directors is included as an essential mechanism of corporate governance, there are many varieties of board structure and function that nonetheless serve similar purposes. The Organisation for Economic Co-operation and Development (OECD) corporate governance principles accept there are different models of corporate governance. For example, they do not advocate any particular board structure and

> the term "board" ... is meant to embrace the different national models of board structures found in OECD and non-OECD countries. In the typical two-tier system, found in some countries, "board" as used in the *Principles* refers to the "supervisory board" while "key

executives" refers to the "management board." In systems where the unitary board is overseen by an internal auditor's body, the principles applicable to the board are also, *mutatis mutandis,* applicable. The terms "corporation" and "company" are used interchangeably.
(OECD 2004: 15)

The size and structure of boards of directors in different regions tend to reflect the perceived role and purpose of the board. In European countries and Japan, the board is viewed as having a representative role as well as a decision-making role involving wide stakeholder interests, as a consequence boards tend to be larger in size (Figure 2.1). In Anglo-American countries, boards of directors are regarded as having more specific purposes and directed towards a more focused range of interests, and therefore tend to be smaller bodies. Some of the different approaches to boards in the different regional corporate governance systems include:

- **US boards**: US boards are unitary and tend to be larger, and traditionally combined with the roles of chair and CEO; there is a predominance of non-executives many of whom traditionally were CEOs of other companies.
- **UK boards**: UK boards are unitary and separate the roles of chair and CEO; non-executives are in a majority; boards are often small particularly in smaller companies.

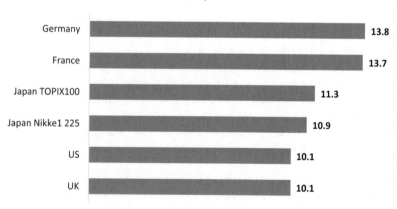

Figure 2.1 International Comparison of Large Listed Company Board Size

- **European boards (Germanic)**: European boards as in the north European German model tend to have two tiers, with stakeholder representation on supervisory boards, but preclude the face-to-face accountability of executives on the management board to board members from outside the company.
- **European boards (Latin)**: European boards of the Latin variety tend to have a large representation of owners and related interests on boards, with little separation of ownership and control.
- **Asian boards**: Asian boards tend to represent dominant family interests, or other majority shareholders, and there is no separation of ownership and control.
- **Japanese boards**: Japanese boards traditionally were large nominal boards composed of executives and former executives of the company; the board performed largely ritualistic procedures to order and was based on long-established relationships. Recent reforms in Japan have introduced independent directors for the first time, but the traditional culture and reserve of Japanese boards often remain in place.

Debate continues in all systems concerning the ideal size, structure, operation, and ultimate purpose of boards of directors, and almost all governance systems around the world have been engaged in a prolonged process of reform and continuous improvement. Whether the essential role of the board is monitoring management or offering strategic leadership, and the interests the board should essentially reflect, is often contested. In the *Principles of Corporate Governance*, the OECD (2004) attempts to tread diplomatically between the alternative views (whilst referring to potential "serious weaknesses" in the European two-tier board system):

> With unitary board systems a tension is sometimes observed between the view that the board should contribute contacts, resources and skills to the operation of the company, and the position that the board is primarily in place to monitor the management. The two views have different implications for the structure of the board, the former arguing for a greater share of insiders relative to outsiders. The *Principles* make a more nuanced case by specifying that the board is chiefly responsible for monitoring managerial performance and achieving an adequate rate of return for shareholders, while preventing conflicts of interest and balancing competing demands on the company. Most important of all, the board is responsible for guiding corporate strategy. In two tier board systems, the

question of composition does not arise (i.e. the supervisory board is by law non-executive) although the degree to which it can and should guide corporate strategy and balance interests is often debated. Also debated is whether the absence of executives limits their access to information and restrains informed debate, and at the end of the day could lead to ineffective monitoring. This is an issue in Germany, leading the authorities to introduce a self-check system for supervisory boards.

(OECD 2004)

Davies and Hopt (2013) in their consideration of board accountability and convergence are more critical of the monitoring capacity of the German supervisory board structure, compared to the more robust monitoring of the UK board structure (though placing the emphasis perhaps on financial monitoring rather than the production and product focus of German boards). The OECD is also critical of what it suggests in the "unwieldy size" of supervisory boards and supported the European Union in offering companies the choice of one or two-tier systems for companies registering under European statutes (*societas europeaea*). In debating the advantages and disadvantages of the two systems, the OECD (2004) inclines towards the French support of two systems, and Italian system offering three choices of board structure. In an OECD (2021: 14) international survey of corporate governance practice, the growing number of jurisdictions that allow either one-tier or two-tier boards is recognised, but the emphasis is put upon the importance of significant representation of independent directors in both systems of boards, and particularly independent audit committees.

Roles of Boards in Financial Disclosure

A major responsibility of the board of directors is to ensure shareholders and stakeholders are provided with high-quality disclosures on the financial and operating results of the company, and on company objectives, so that they may make informed and accurate assessments of the progress of the company. Almost all of the corporate governance codes around the world, including the OECD (2015b) principles, *Sarbanes–Oxley Act* (2002), UK *Code* (2014), and EU *Transparency Directive* (2004), emphasise the importance of full disclosure as the vital basis for the effective working of all of the other mechanisms of corporate governance. UNCTAD (2006) has distilled these collected guidelines into requirements on financial disclosures, and on company objectives. With regard to financial disclosures, UNCTAD (2006: 3) states:

The quality of financial disclosures depends significantly on the robustness of the financial reporting standards on the basis of which the financial information is prepared and reported. In most circumstances, the financial reporting standards required for corporate reporting are contained in the generally accepted principles recognised in the country where the entity is domiciled. Over the last few decades, there has been increasing convergence towards a set of non-jurisdiction specific, widely recognised financial reporting standards. The *International Financial Reporting Standards* (IFRSs) issued by the International Accounting Standards Board provide a widely recognised benchmark in this respect. Furthermore, the board of directors could enrich the usefulness of the disclosures on the financial and operating results of a company by providing further explanation for example in the Management's Discussion and Analysis section of the company in addition to the disclosure required by the applicable financial reporting standards. The board could clearly identify inherent risks and estimates used in the preparation and reporting of the financial and operating results of the company in order to give investors a better understanding of the risks they are taking in relying on the judgement of management.

With reference to disclosure of company objectives, UNCTAD recognises two general categories of company objectives: fundamental objectives that seek to answer the basic question of "why does the company exist?" and secondly more basic commercial objectives. Included among the essential non-financial disclosures of company objectives are

- ownership and shareholder rights;
- changes in control and transactions involving significant assets;
- governance structures and policies;
- members of the board and key executives;
- material issues regarding stakeholders, and environmental and social stewardship;
- material foreseeable risk factors;
- independence of external auditors; and
- internal audit function.

The traditional practice of including all of this disclosure in annual company reports has now been largely superseded by the imperative for continuous disclosure, demanded by both markets and regulators. Today boards of directors of major corporations are required to continually consider carefully their responsibilities for disclosure of any significant matters that come before the board, for example, of anticipated merger and takeover activity, even if this may involve a temporary suspension of trading in the company shares. At such junctures, the board's responsibilities for accountability and strategy may collide.

Roles of Boards in Strategy

In determining the strategic role of the board, the academic literature has presented contrasting views. With the obsessive focus of agency theory on the monitoring role of the firm this perspective as Pugliese and Zattoni (2012: 218) observe, "Direct involvement of board members into strategy is not expected, as it would (i) impose boards of directors to be co-responsible for strategic decisions, and (ii) reduce the required distance between board members and managers" (Sundaramurthy and Lewis, 2003). In contrast, other perspectives have a more positive view of the contribution the board may make to corporate strategy "various theories (e.g. stewardship, resource dependency, and resource-based view) foster the idea that boards are organisational bodies that may support empowered managers in strategy formulation and implementation" (Bezemer, 2010) (Pugliese and Zattoni (2012: 219).

As Pugliese and Satomi (2012: 221) maintain:

> boards are becoming more actively involved in strategy (Zahra and Filatotchev, 2004). Boards have affected important elements of strategies, such as the scope of the firm (Tihanyi et al., 2003), entrepreneurship and innovation (Fried et al.,1998; Zahra et al., 2000; Hoskisson et al., 2002), strategic change (Westphal and Fredrickson, 2001), R&D strategies, and internationalization (Sanders and Carpenter 1998).

Board of directors' involvement in strategy may be operationalised in a number of ways:

- boards may be expected to participate to general strategy and decision-making (including defining the mission and vision of the company
- boards may contribute to shaping specific strategic outcomes (which might include internationalisation of operations, corporate entrepreneurship, diversification, or restructuring for example)
- boards may take part in various phases of the strategic decision-making processes, whether by identification of the most appropriate

strategic direction, ratification, implementation, or evaluation (Pugliese et al. 2009; Pugliese and Zattoni 2012: 221)

In normal circumstances, boards do not pursue strategies of their own and act in concert with executive management in developing strategy.

> Corporate entrepreneurship is the result of interactions between board members and the TMT (Zahra et al., 2009). Boards' contribution occurs through continuative actions and interactions with managers; henceforth, collaboration, empowerment and trust should be considered as key drivers of effective innovation activities.
>
> (Pugliese and Zattoni 2012: 226)

(However, at times of company crisis [the responsibility for which is attributed to the incumbent executive management] it is sometimes necessary for the board of directors to seize the reins of power, if only to install a new executive management.)

The competitive challenges that companies face and need to devise strategies to succeed in are complex, and the composition and talents of boards are diverse, and therefore the strategic role that boards may play and how they play this is difficult to define in advance. As Pugliese and Zattoni (2012: 226) conclude:

> Overall, while there is an agreement in terms of boards' primary function in shaping firm innovation and corporate entrepreneurship, there is a dearth of clarity with regard to the type of activities that should be pursued by board members. Strategic decision-making and entrepreneurial actions are the result of a process that requires involvement, skills and knowledge from the participants aside from the monetary incentives. According to resource-based views of the firm, boards act as a catalyst of knowledge and resources necessary to support managers in defining the strategic posture (Zahra et al., 2009). Aside from this view, empowerment, trust and collaboration between (outside) board members and insiders is crucial to determine positive choices in terms of entrepreneurial activities.
>
> (Gabrielsson 2007)

Inevitably though, boards of directors will be involved in strategy in some way, as Harvey-Jones rhetorically asks: "If the board is not taking the company purposefully into the future who is?" (1998: 162). But it is difficult to ascertain what is an appropriate level of involvement.

Table 2.2 Typology of Directors

Executive directors	Knowledge of day-to-day operations; communicate and implement decisions	Management nexus focused
Non-executive ('outside') directors	Strategy; continuity; expertise	Long-term planning; oversight of key risk areas
'Independent' directors	Perspective; objectivity	Conflict-sensitive functions

Source: Adapted from: Kirkpatrick Grant (2004), '*Typology of Directors' Policy Dialogue on Corporate Governance in China,*' presentation Shanghai, 25 February, Paris: OECD.

Sarah Hogg chair of 3i, one of the most strategically innovative companies in the FTSE 100, commented, "Indisputably, this is a board function, but how is strategy set? Where do strategic discussions end and management responsibilities begin?" and argues, "The need to see the board's strategic responsibilities as long-term, aspirational, and qualitative, in contrast to short term budget-setting or competitive strategies" (Cadbury 2002: xii). There is a distinction between the long-term oversight of strategy that is rightly the board's responsibility, and the creation and implementation of strategies which is the role of executive management (Table 2.2).

It is the formulation and endorsement of strategy that the board can be at its most cohesive, as Stiles and Taylor argue:

> Close working between the executive and non-executive cadres promotes enhanced strategic discussion, greater information flow between members, and a lack of dominance of any one individual or sub-group over the board as a whole. One major problem with the adversarial view is that it downplays the role boards can play in the strategy process and in shaping the identity of the organization ... Board involvement in the strategy process entails a much higher degree of collaboration between executives and non-executives and in a real sense a relaxing of the constraints of independence in order for trust to be generated and social cohesion to be established.
>
> (2002: 2)

As with the conduct of other board duties, however, there is a gradation of engagement in strategic involvement, from passive boards that adopt a minimalist approach to their statutory duties, to boards that adopt a review and approve stance, to boards that do seek for an active partnership with executive management in establishing the strategic direction of the enterprise.

A strategic board is one that contributes to the leadership and direction of the business through a mix of monitoring and supportive behaviours vis-à-vis executives. Non-executives need to be continuously active in respect of both strategy process (how strategy is developed) and strategy content (the substance of choice, change and risk involved in corporate strategy). There is a strong consensus that responsibility for developing strategy rests with the chief executive, in concert with his/her executive committee. Non-executives then make an important contribution by bringing to bear experience and knowledge gained outside the organisation, to challenge and test both the overarching strategic framework of the business as well as specific proposals for strategic investment, divestment, and change (McNulty et al., 2003: 2).

The Development of Law and Regulation

As corporations developed within market economies, a framework of law and regulation has evolved to bring order to their activities, to maintain competition, and to ensure fair treatment of those who interact with corporations. In each country and region, a set of laws, regulations, stock-exchange listing requirements, and voluntary practices together provides the basis for corporate governance. These institutions and relations are derived from the history, culture, and economic circumstances of particular societies (Frentrop 2003). Three legal fields are relevant to the existence and operation of corporate governance according to Aglietta and Reberioux (2005):

1 *Financial market regulation*: Comprises all regulations covering share issues (primary capital markets) and subsequent transactions (secondary capital markets), which aim to reduce information asymmetries between investors and insiders of the company, to prevent misappropriation of value by inside players (Black 2001). Firstly, regulation aims to increase financial transparency, and ensure disclosure of information, and secondly insider trading and internal transactions are prohibited.

2 *Corporate law*: Comprises the legal rules defining the relationships between different constituents of the company, including shareholders, directors, managers, and employees. Company law deals with the rights of shareholdings, including voting rights, the power

of general meetings of shareholders, the composition and func-
tioning of the board, the accountability of managers and directors, and the legitimate objectives and purposes of the company.
3 *Labour law*: Labour law directly affects corporate governance
when it legislates for worker involvement in decision-making processes. This can range from negotiated involvement in the firm
through its supervisory body or collective bargaining processes,
to consultative involvement. Codetermination as practised in
Germany may be part of positive rights which induce managers
to take the interests of employees into account when making decisions (Streeck 2001; Aglietta and Reberioux 2005: 54).

The US legal structure is dedicated to achieving market liquidity
and shareholder value with highly developed securities market law to
impose disclosure of information to the capital markets. The Securities and Exchange Commission (SEC) regulates the capital markets,
supervising the value chain, including harmonising the accounting
standards, auditing, and financial analysis. In contrast, corporate law
is developed by the individual states in the US, with competition to
attract company registrations, with Delaware dominating in this regulatory competition. Companies therefore have a degree of flexibility
in their corporate governance. The performance of fiduciary duties by
directors is reinforced by the high risk of litigation. Yet, there is some
controversy regarding the nature of fiduciary duties, and it is argued
these should be exercised in the interests of the shareholders and the
company. This legal framework allows managers significant room to
manoeuvre (Aglietta and Reberioux 2005: 56).

The German model of governance and law traditionally appeared
the direct opposite of the US, with financial market law specific to
each state, undeveloped capital markets, and highly concentrated
ownership. Financial transparency is lower, and banks play a more
direct intermediary role, acting simultaneously in the role of suppliers
of credit, share owners, and proxy holders for the voting rights of their
customers, as well as members of the supervisory board. In contrast,
federal corporate law regulates the internal organisation of companies,
with a dual structure, of board of directors (*Vorstand*) and a supervisory board (*Aufsichtsrat*). The codetermination system is guaranteed
by both corporate and labour law at the federal level, with worker representatives joining shareholder representatives on the supervisory
board. This whole system is designed to integrate compromise in German companies between the interests of shareholders, management,
workers, and creditors. This strong procedural integration internally

has the corollary of weak transparency and capital market liquidity externally (Aglietta and Reberioux 2005: 57).

In France, capital markets are more developed and regulated by the Commission des Operations de Bourse (COB) modelled on the SEC. As in Germany, corporate governance is regulated more by corporate law than financial markets law. There is the possibility of a dual structure board, though most companies have a single structure, the dualistic structure is adopted by some large companies. Employee involvement is less in Germany but exists through consultation in the works council, and since the councils have some rights of professional advice and legal redress, it does represent an element of co-supervision. As with the German system, in French law, there is a holistic sense of the company as an autonomous entity with a corporate interest, as articulated in the Vienot I (1995) report on corporate governance commissioned by French Business Confederation (MEDEF) and the French Association of Private Businesses (AFEP) (Aglietta and Reberioux 2005: 59). The Vienot report states:

> In Anglo-Saxon countries, the emphasis is primarily placed on the objectives of fast maximization of share value, whereas, on the European continent in general and in France in particular, it is placed rather on the corporate interest of the company ... The corporate interest can be defined as the greater interest of the body itself, in other words the company considered as an autonomous economic agent pursuing its own ends, distinct notably from those of its shareholders, employees, creditors (including the tax authorities), suppliers and customers, but which correspond to their common general interest, which is to ensure prosperity and continuity of the company.
>
> (1995: 8)

From this comparison, a further characterisation of the two major competing systems of corporate governance based on their regulatory structures and the related distinctive conceptions of the firm is possible:

- The US approach has a resolutely favourable orientation to shareholders through strong regulation of capital markets. High disclosure requirements are maintained, along with intervention by the SEC. In contrast, corporate law regarding direct regulation of intra-firm relations is weak. Formal integration of employees into decision-making does not exist, but informal cultural integration may occur. The distribution of power regarding the ultimate destiny of the firm is assumed to rest with the external shareholders, with a property rights conception of the firm prevailing, and fairly immediate and measurable shareholder value assumed to be the major driver.

- The continental European approach has less emphasis on capital markets, which have traditionally been less important in this system, and favours internal regulation of the firm. Corporate and labour law plays a much greater role in orchestrating the deliberative structures between the main participants in the firm. The controlling interests of majority shareholders protect management from capital market fluctuations. A holistic, partnership-based conception of the firm prevails, expressed in commitments to the corporate interest and worker involvement, with the major driver being the generation of sustained company value to be distributed among all participants and the wider community (Aglietta and Reberioux 2005: 59).

The slightly unreal sense of the European approach to corporate governance, compared with the sharp ring of reality regarding the US approach to corporate governance, reflects the extraordinary ascendancy of the US model since the 1990s with the industrial renaissance of the New Economy there. Yet as recently as the 1980s, it was apparent that the traditional manufacturing-based US economy could not compete with the Japanese or German industry (Porter 1992) and was in decline.

Structural weaknesses in the US approach to corporate governance caused this competitive failure, including the precedence given to finance capital with the high rate of interest extracted from industrial concerns, causing the erosion of strategic investment in organisational capability (Lazonick 1992: 480), the failure to adequately accept "the collective nature of human endeavour" (Piore 2004: 142), and the essential basis of team production (Blair and Stout 1999; Blair 2004). Though a new institutional accommodation may have been constructed in the 1990s around newer industries and technologies in the US, whether this will have any longevity remains to be seen. Nonetheless, the US approach as manifest by the most powerful economy at the centre of global financial systems has until now often exercised what has seemed at times an almost hegemonic influence upon the international corporate governance system.

Bank, Majority, and Market-Based Finance

Related closely to the development of law and regulation in corporate governance is the issue of corporate finance. From where a company derives the finance it requires to develop and grow is one of the most fundamental questions any enterprise faces. The two principal ways of raising external finance are through bank finance or equity finance by selling shares on the stock market. Once this critical choice between alternative sources of finance is made, there are profound implications for the governance structures resulting. Williamson argues, "Debt and equity are treated not mainly as alternative financial instruments, but rather as alternative governance structures. Debt governance works mainly out of rules, while equity governance allows much greater discretion" (1998: 567).

The evolution of capital markets is divided by Rybczynski (1997) into three phases, bank-oriented, market-oriented, and securitised. Though at each stage banks remain responsible for payments services and liquidity, over time there is adjustment in the allocation of saving, monitoring, and disciplining of users of external finance, and in the management of risk. In the bank phase, the external funding of firms is obtained from banks in the form of loans, with banks monitoring the performance of borrowers. In this phase, banks play a dominant role in the economy as financial intermediaries, and may in some markets hold equity stakes in firms. In the market-oriented phase, banks face competition from other providers of financial products, with the growth of the institutional investors, and individual holdings of securities. Banks remain the major source of external funding for firms, but money and capital markets begin to develop. As other sources of external finance develop, monitoring begins to be shared with the other financial institutions. In the third securitisation phase, the market provides most finance to firms, and also to the financial sector. Corporate bonds and commercial paper replace bank loans, and mortgages and consumer credit are securitised. Allocating savings and monitoring is undertaken by the financial markets through rating agencies, investment banks, and institutional investors. New financial products are developed such as derivatives that allow pricing and trading of risks, and new financial expertise emerges (Davis 2000: 3–4).

Historically, the evolution of capital markets has proceeded at a different pace regionally, and the result is a varying emphasis on the importance of different kinds of finance and the related governance structures. Davis (1996, 2002) elaborates the distinctions arriving out of different financing into four paradigms of corporate governance:

- direct control via debt
- market control via equity
- market control via debt
- direct control via equity

Direct Control via Debt

This governance system is associated with Germany and Japan, where a close relationship is maintained with a small number of creditors and equity holders, and monitoring is delegated to the bank as a trusted intermediary. Wide crossholding of shares exist among companies, with banks themselves as significant shareholders, and in Germany having a substantial presence on supervisory boards as both equity holders and creditors. Bank influence is further increased by being able to exert control over the voting rights of individual investors who have transferred their proxies. The influence of other shareholders, including other institutions, is limited by voting restrictions, the strong countervailing influence of other corporate shareholders, and the lack of disclosure of detailed financial information, combined with the formal rights to board representation of other stakeholders including employees, suppliers, and creditors.

Market Control via Equity

This is the governance system ideally associated with the UK and the US, in which greater dependence on equity finance by companies involves disclosure to the market of widely dispersed shareholders who may exercise influence by buying or selling shares on liquid equity markets that reward performing companies with higher share prices, and sanction poorly performing companies with lower share prices, that make them more vulnerable, including to the possibility of takeover. Takeover activity is the most dramatic way of resolving apparent conflicts between management orientations and shareholders' interests:

> Those firms which deviate most extensively from shareholders' objectives – and which consequently tend to have lower market values as shareholders dispose of their holdings – have a greater likelihood of being acquired. The threat of takeover, as much as its manifestation, acts as a constraint on managerial behaviour. Institutional shareholders, both directly and via non-executive directors can have an important role to play in this context both in complementing takeover pressures as a monitoring constraint on management behaviour, and in evaluating takeover proposals when they do arise.
>
> (Davis 1996: 83)

Market Control via Debt

In the past, takeovers were resorted to normally in very particular circumstances where either an incumbent management was clearly slipping or the synergies to be released from a takeover were apparently too great to resist. However, in the 1980s, this all changed with the arrival of junk bonds: bonds issued by companies considered to be higher credit risks, considered speculative rather than investment grade, with a higher chance of default than other bonds. Banks and institutions now joined in to finance highly leveraged takeovers through the issue of a vast amount of junk bonds. Debt was seen as a way of reasserting control on managers, since without internal resources, they needed to return to the market either for further debt or equity capital or for any new initiative (Jensen 1986). One disadvantage of loading companies with debt though was that directors and shareholders in highly leveraged firms might have an incentive to engage in high-risk projects, since under limited liability, their creditors would bear most of the cost if the venture was unsuccessful. Disenchantment with highly leveraged takeovers set in with an increase in the bankruptcy rate, the diversion of management energies engaging in takeover and defence strategies, the panoply of defence mechanisms from takeover erected across the corporate sector, and the onset of recession at the end of the 1980s.

Direct Control via Equity

Searching for a more positive way of monitoring and influencing management of corporations in the 1990s onwards, the investment institutions have launched a corporate governance movement to restore the traditional rights of shareholders to elect the board of directors and influence the choice of strategic policies of management. Formal and informal engagement with management by major institutions has developed, and the sophistication of institutional investor corporate governance policies increased. Indexing strategies by leading institutional investors force funds to hold shares in companies that observe certain policies. Most institutions prefer to stay with the index, but even active investors who try to achieve greater influence in selective investment strategies need to consider the significant cost in disposing of shareholdings, and are often driven to further increase their control over companies due to the illiquidity of the market (Davis 1996: 84).

However, there is a fifth paradigm for financing and governance of enterprises, which is more universal than the other approaches, and often co-exists with them, and that is *Managerial Control via Retained Earnings*. In all governance systems, most of the finance for expansion and innovation comes through the growth in the revenue of companies, and the retention of these earnings for further investment. This organic approach to capital investment is the essential well-spring of the corporate system. Of course, this internal source of finance buttresses the position of the incumbent management, though it can be argued they are in the best position to judge both the need for new investment in the company, and the most appropriate means of raising finance. This approach until recently at least has fared better in the German and Japanese systems. However, despite the repeated strenuous efforts to incorporate more energetic market disciplines, the use of retained earnings for investment has remained central to the Anglo-American model also, as Bill Lazonick insists:

> The financial basis of innovative strategies in the United States has always been, and remains, retained earnings. For strategic management of going concerns, retained earnings permit new investments in organization and technology to be financed without incurring legal obligations to pay returns. Retained earnings represent low-cost finance, and control over retained earnings is the quintessential mode of securing financial commitment. In addition, a stream of retained earnings can be used to pay the interest charges on investments that are externally financed. Depending on projected sales revenues, earnings retention, and bond rates, strategic management can choose a debt-equity ratio that leverages retained earnings without jeopardizing the financial ability of the firm to implement its investment strategy.
>
> (1992: 457)

Lazonick argues that contrary to economic folklore, common share issues have never been important to US industry to finance business expansion, and in contrast to the large volume of bond issues, new share issues have been responsible for only a small proportion of the capital raised in the US (Taggart 1986; Lazonick 1992: 457). New share issues essentially gained their prominence from owner-entrepreneurs taking their firms public. Beyond that, share issues have been significant more recently for acquisition and restructuring strategies. Finally, much of the recent frenzied attention given to equity markets is the result of the arrival of stock options as the primary form of executive compensation in the US which over time switched managers' focus from the performance of their company in product markets to their share performance in equity markets:

> The ability of managers to buy stocks at a discount transformed career employees into substantial owners. The exercise of stock options meant a stream of dividends if the managers held onto the

stocks, or, in a rising market, capital gains if the managers (usually after a restricted period) sold the stocks. Ownership income began to dwarf compensation income for top managers ... With capital gains income over twenty times dividend income, and hence constituting the bulk of their total income, the lesson for top managers who were motivated by such matters ... was to prevent even short-run declines in the market value of their companies' stocks. Strategic managers of industrial corporations joined the money managers of institutional portfolios in focusing on the bottom line of their companies' quarterly reports.

(Lazonick 1992: 462)

Despite the way equity markets have seized the public attention in recent decades, a final form of governance and finance remains the most popular in large parts of the world, that is *Direct Control via Majority Group.*

Majority Group Control

As extensive research by La Porta et al. (1999) and Claessens et al. (2000) demonstrate the most prevalent form of control over companies throughout the world is not market control but direct control by majority groups. Even in Japan and Germany where bank influence has been greatest, this was heavily supported by large crossholding of shares between enterprises. In other countries, the majority shareholders are often family members, often with one figure in a dominant ownership and control position. The OECD comments:

It is commonly accepted that the structure of ownership in the US and the UK is widely dispersed while in other countries the situation is one of concentrated ownership. This picture is, however, somewhat exaggerated. While the median largest voting block in these two countries is 10 per cent or less and 30–60 per cent in other countries, there are also a number of companies with very concentrated voting power ... As in other countries these companies often reflect the dominance of a family holding. Much the same pattern emerges when considering the second and third largest voting blocks, with the UK rather more similar to Europe than to the US.

(2004: 18)

Who the majority shareholders are also differs widely with financial institutions important in many countries with the exception of France.

The nature of the major institutional influence is also different with pension funds very important in the US and the UK. The importance of banks in Japan needs to be qualified by the fact that insurance companies are the banks' own major shareholders. With regard to the non-financial sector, individuals are dominant in the US but in most other countries, except the UK, it is other companies that tend to have crossholding of shares in each other. This reflects the prevalence of, and commitment to, company groups in many countries. The OECD continues:

> Groups of companies are often associated with particular con-trol devices such as pyramids and cross shareholdings. One study examined 2890 companies in Europe finding that nearly 30 per cent of them were in the third or lower down layers but that a third also showed no deviation of cash flow from voting rights. The lowest deviation for the average cash to voting rights ratio was in the UK while there were large deviations in Belgium, France and Germany, with a rather complex picture emerging for Italy. In Italy the governance system is characterised by voice rather than by exit of the important shareholders. Powerful families, finan-cial holding companies and cross shareholdings are a common feature. Corporate networks, voting agreements and hierarchical groups, especially in Belgium, France and Italy, are a device for concentrating voting power without concentrating ownership and cash flow rights. They also shield the controlling group from hos-tile take-overs. However, they also open the system to abuse of minority shareholders.
>
> (2004: 19)

Bratton and McCahery (2002) contrast the relative merits of the mar-ket and majority ownership system (which they characterise as block-holding systems, with majority or near-majority holdings of stock in the hands of one, two, or a small group of large investors). They refer to how widely dispersed shareholding prevents close monitoring of management, but go on to insist:

> Market systems have countervailing advantages. Their sharehold-ers cheaply can reduce their risk through diversification. Relative to shareholders in blockholder systems, they receive high rates of return. The systems' deep trading markets facilitate greater share-holder liquidity. These capital markets also facilitate corporate finance, providing management with greater flexibility as to the

type and sources of new capital than do markets in blockholder systems. More generally, they provide an environment relatively more conducive to management entrepreneurship, as reflected in increased investment in new technologies. Finally, although market system shareholders and their outside-director agents cannot access full information about firm operations, their very distance from operations yields a countervailing benefit. Distance makes them relatively immune to capture by the management interest and assures objective evaluation of the information they do receive. A practice of objective evaluation means relatively fewer barriers to disinvestment and related features of downside restructuring.

(2002: 26)

Concentrated ownership offers a different set of advantages:

Blockholder systems, like market systems, leave management in charge of the business plan and operations. But large-block investments imply a closer level of shareholder monitoring. In addition, the coalescence of voting power in a small number of hands means earlier, cheaper intervention in the case of management failure. The systems' other primary benefit stems from the blockholders' ability to access information about operations. This lessened information asymmetry permits block-holders to invest more patiently. The longer shareholder time-horizon in turn frees management to invest for a long term and creates a more secure environment for firm-specific investments of human capital by the firm's managers.

(2002: 27)

Concentrated ownership has survived in most countries of the world as the most common form of ownership and control, and whatever its limitations, retains the greatest influence in the corporate governance systems of most countries. However, in the two most powerful economies associated with this form of governance, Germany and Japan, questions have been raised concerning the central role assumed to be played by the banks. Roe (1994) examined the monitoring practice of banks in Germany, and though he found significant bank shareholdings and governance input, this did not involve an activist role in investment and divestment policies, and banks tend to act in a largely lender's role. Gorton and Schmid (1996) suggest the role of German bank monitoring has changed over time, and that earlier there were firm performance improvements depending on how much equity banks owned, though this changed by the 1980s. Baums (1998) argues though the banks held a significant place in the German system of corporate governance, with just three of the largest banks holding 37 of 231 positions reserved for stockholders in the supervisory boards of the 24 non-financial companies which composed the DAX 30 in 1998, their real influence was limited by the personal interlocks between the publicly listed firms and the co-determination regime. Baums insists real influence was in the hands of a small number of individuals who controlled more than half the positions available on the boards of DAX 30 companies.

Equally the relationships in Japan are more complex than simply bank lenders acting as idealised shareholder monitors. Aoki (1990) suggests that before the long economic crisis of Japan commencing in the early 1990s, the system involved interdependencies between vertically related non-financial firms, non-hierarchical management practices, and a highly articulated incentive structure that included the norm of lifetime employment in the major corporations. Japanese banks did play a key role in providing substantial funds to firms, allowing investment plans to proceed with diminished sensitivity to internal cash flow (Hoshi et al., 1991). If this allowed sustained growth during the long Japanese march to overwhelm overseas markets, continuing expansionary lending when opportunities and cash flow were drying up as the bubble was about to burst could not have helped the corporations they were supposed to be monitoring. When attention turns as in Germany, to the role of industrial crossholding of shares in the Japanese *keiretsus*, the purpose of these was largely to stabilise long-term relational contracts among members of vertical production groups, rather than to exercise any monitoring function (Bratton and McCahery 1999).

Many commentators have argued there will a be a gradual unwinding of majority group control at least in the leading industrial countries as equity markets deepen, as institutions continue to grow and invest overseas, and as national regulation becomes less benign towards group formation and existence. There has been a rapid growth of the number of listed companies in France, Germany, and Spain, and a remarkable growth in market capitalisation across all European markets. A significant measure of the scale of this growth is stock market capitalisation as a percentage of Gross Domestic Product, which in the Netherlands is approaching US and UK levels. In Germany, the 50 per cent capital gains tax on the sale of shares, which locked financial institutions into their web of crossholding of shares, was abolished in 2002, and created the possibility of reducing vast blocks of shares and precipitating merger and acquisition activity and shareholder activism (Coffee 2002).

The rapid and sustained growth of capitalisation in the stock markets of Europe at least will unsettle the established groups and networks of the past. Davis and Steil argue:

> In corporate finance, major changes are in prospect as institutions impact on bank-based systems of corporate governance ... European and Japanese financial systems are likely to shift to an Anglo-Saxon paradigm under pressure from institutionalization, although the processes will be slow.
>
> (2000: 6)

Yet the institutional and cultural differences which persist, and the complementarities that make these different systems both coherent and viable, are a resilient manifestation of *path dependence* in the view of Bebchuk and Roe (2004). While insistent market pressures may cause changes to occur, enduring institutional complementarities will survive.

The Market for Corporate Control

The market for corporate control whereby a company perceived to be not performing well, or to have hidden assets which were not being utilised, could be put into play, is one of the most severe disciplinary mechanisms in the market-based model of corporate governance. Though always present, this was a particularly brutal restraining influence on management in the US in the 1970s and 1980s whether it was the threat of a takeover bid, or cash, or leveraged buyout. Such takeovers usually involved both the removal of the incumbent management and the radical restructuring of the company to release the revenue to meet the cost of the takeover.

> While merger and acquisition activity in the 1980s positively restructured some overextended conglomerates, it also had a downside. It was associated with reductions in plant and R&D expenditures, showed no net positive effects on productivity, and did not have clear efficiency advantages once its redistributional elements (from incumbent employees to shareholders) were factored into the analysis.
>
> (Jacoby 2002: 18)

Yet, even in the 1980s, takeover rates rarely exceeded 1.5 per cent (the number of bids as a percentage of the number of listed companies) and they declined steeply later. Moreover, only 4 per cent of all US deals were hostile, suggesting the threat of hostile takeover was greater than the reality (Becht et al., 2003: 70). However, by the 1990s, with the help of the courts, corporate management had erected a series of defences against takeovers. In marked contrast, takeovers were a comparatively rare event in Europe, and hostile takeovers unheard of, particularly in Germany.

With the new found enthusiasm for equity markets in Europe in the 1990s and 2000s, corporate takeovers became a more widespread and aggressive phenomenon throughout the continent. Occasionally the most publicised takeovers involved US or UK corporations such as General Motors acquiring half ownership of Saab in 1989, or Ford Motors' takeover of Volvo Motors in 1999. The largest hostile takeover threatened in German industrial history occurred in 2000 when the UK mobile phone group Vodafone bid $199 billion for Mannesmann which shocked the German public and led to a broad debate on the future of the German model of capitalism.

German trade unions and the Mannesmann works councils strongly rejected Vodafone's bid, in order to defend the German culture of corporate governance which is based on strong employee involvement and co-determination. With the employees' viewpoint supported by almost all major political parties in Germany, Vodafone reacted to the criticism by saying that, after a takeover of Mannesmann, it would fully accept the German system of industrial relations and corporate governance (see Case Study 7). In fact, there is a long history of European companies taking over Anglo-American companies including Daimler's takeover of Chrysler in 1998, and for example Blumberg reports in 2014 there were 709 European takeovers of US companies worth a total of $140 billion proposed, compared with 835 proposed deals for $183 billion in which US companies were the intended buyers of European businesses (Bershidsky 2014).

Hostile takeovers were also experienced within European countries, in Italy with the bids of Olivetti for Telecom Italia; and Generali for INA; and in France with the bids of BNP for Paribas; and Elf Aquitaine for Total Fina. As European companies which had always been active acquiring companies outside Europe began bidding for each other with greater enthusiasm, the number of takeovers increased significantly in the 1990s, but never reached the frequency experienced in the US and the UK. This provoked questions regarding managerial accountability and the nature of the firm (Deakin and Slinger 1997). A protracted debate in the European Community on the *Takeover Bid Directive* reflected differing conceptions of the firm, with the liberal conception of the firm belonging to the shareholders, opposed by the continental conception of the company as a community, with management obliged to act in the wider corporate interest (Aglietta and Reberioux 2005: 67).

In the end, the *Takeover Bid Directive* text left considerable freedom for member states to make their own choice of rules regarding takeovers. In France, a series of reforms in 2001 eased the path of takeovers, though not entirely as the law established an obligation to inform and consult with the works council of targeted firms. In Germany, there was a strengthening of anti-takeover devices, as though accepting a takeover becomes obligatory when a shareholder exceeds a threshold of 30 per cent of voting rights, the law allowed managers to erect takeover defences as long as this occurred before any bid took place. The role of the supervisory board is increased during takeovers, and the works council is required to be informed by both sides (Aglietta and Reberioux 2005: 70). It appears that with regard to takeover regulation, a specifically European solution is emerging. However, hostile mergers and acquisitions continue internationally within a range of $3–$4 trillion annually.

In conclusion, regarding the impact of different modes of financing, Aglietta and Reberioux (2001) conceive of three corporate governance regimes, which may coexist and compete with each other: internal control, majority group control, and market control (Table 3.1). In a later formulation (2005), they elaborate the three regimes as: *Internal control* involves control by banks and constraint by debt, with the dominant strategy being internal growth resulting in the entrenchment of technocratic managers. *Majority shareholding group control* involves an alliance between majority shareholders, managers, and institutional investors. While institutional investors rely on governance charters, majority shareholders can exert influence through the board of directors. For the two kinds of investors, the dominant strategy is return on equity capital. *Control by the stock market* is the third regime, with a dominant strategy as the maximisation of market value through external growth, and to protect the company from takeover bids. The success of one of these forms of control over the others depends on the dominant financial logic:

> The performance of the firm is determined by the interdependencies between the strategy of the managerial team and the financial partners ... The firm has relations with three types of financial agents: the banks, which are assumed to represent all credit

markets; the controlling group of shareholders; and the shareholders and potential inventors who are preoccupied by the dividend yield and the liquidity of their shares. The firm pursues its own objectives, which are those of its managers. The firm is not the agent of any principal. However it takes into account the constraints imposed by the financial players. Its objectives are those which enable the managers to perpetuate their power. The growth of the firm through the investment of its profit is the primary source of this power. Nonetheless, the threat of the market for corporate control obliges managers to concern themselves with their survival.

(Aglietta and Reberioux 2005: 85)

This impelling financial logic continuously encounters robust institutions that are founded on very different principles, and the next chapter considers these profound cultural encounters.

References

Aglietta, M. and Rebérioux, A. (2005) *Corporate Governance Adrift: A Critique of Shareholder Value*, Cheltenham: Edward Elgar.

Aoki, M. (1990) *Information, Incentives and Bargaining in the Japanese Economy: A Micro-Theory of the Japanese Economy*, Cambridge: Cambridge University Press.

Baums, T. (1998) *Corporate Governance in Germany: System and Current Developments*, https://core.ac.uk/download/pdf/14504627.pdf in K.J. Hopt, H. Kanda. M.J. Roe, E. Wymeersch and S. Prigge (eds), *Comparative Corporate Governance: The State of the Art and Emerging Research*, Oxford: Oxford University Press, 545–564.

Bebchuk, L.A., and Roe, M.J. (2004) A Theory of Path Dependence in Corporate Governance and Ownership, in J. N. Gordon and M.J. Roe (eds.), *Convergence and Persistence in Corporate Governance* (pp. 69–95), Cambridge: Cambridge University Press.

Becht, M., Bolton, P. and Röell, A. (2003) Corporate Governance and Control, *Handbook of the Economics of Finance*, 1: 1–109.

Bershidsky, L. (2014) Your Inversion is Germany's Takeover, BlumbergView, 23 September 2016.

Bezemer, P.J. (2010) Diffusion of Corporate Governance Beliefs. PhD thesis. Erasmus Research Institute of Management. Rotterdam, the Netherlands Fried, Bruton and Hisrich, 1998.

Black, B. (2001) The Legal and Institutional Preconditions for Strong Securities Markets, *UCLA Law Review*, 48(4): 781–858.

Blair, M.M. (2004) The Neglected Benefits of the Corporate Form: Entity Status and the Separation of Asset Ownership from Control, in A. Grandori (ed.), *Corporate Governance and Firm Organisation: Microfoundations and Structural Forms* (pp. 45–66), Oxford: Oxford University Press.

Blair, M.M. and Stout, L.A. (1999) A Team Production Theory of Corporate Law, *Virginia Law Review*, 85(2): 247–328.

Bratton, W. and McCahery, J. (2002) *Comparative Corporate Governance and Barriers to Global Cross Reference in Corporate Governance Regimes: Convergence and Diversity*, Oxford: Oxford University Press, 23–55.

Bratton, W.W. and McCahery, J.A. (1999) Comparative Corporate Governance and the Theory of the Firm: The Case against Global Cross Reference, *Columbia Journal of Transnational Law*, 38: 213–297.

Cadbury, A. (2002) *Corporate Governance and Chairmanship*, Oxford: Oxford University Press.

Claessens, S., Djankov, S. and Lang, L.H.P. (2000) The Separation of Ownership and Control in East Asian Corporations, *Journal of Financial Economics*, 58(1): 81–112.

Clarke, T. (2005) Accounting for Enron: Shareholder Value and Stakeholder Interests, *Corporate Governance an International Review*, Blackwell, 13(5): September, 598–613.

Coffee, J. (2002) Convergence and Its Critics: What are the Preconditions to the Separation of Ownership and Control?, in J.A. McCahery, P. Moerland, T. Raaijmakers and L. Renneboog (eds.), *Corporate Governance Regimes: Convergence and Diversity*, Oxford: Oxford University Press.

Davies, P. and Hopt, K. (2013) Corporate Boards in Europe – Accountability and Convergence, *The American Journal of Comparative Law*, 61(2): 301–375.

Davis, E.P. (1996) *The Role of Institutional Investors in the Evolution of Financial Structure and Behaviour*, in The Future of the Financial System, Proceedings of a Conference Held in the Reserve Bank of Australia, Sydney, and Financial Markets Group Special Paper, 89, London School of Economics.

Davis, E.P. (2000) *Implications of the Growth of Institutional Investors for the Financial Sectors*, Discussion Paper PI-0001, Pensions Institute, Birkbeck College, University of London, http://www.pensions-institute.org/

Davis, E.P. (2002) *Institutional Investors, Corporate Governance, and the Peformance of the Corporate Sector*, Middlesex: Brunel University.

Davis, E.P. and Steil, B. (2000) *Institutional Investors*, Boston: MIT Press.

Deakin, S. and Slinger, G. (1997) Hostile Takeovers, Corporate Law, and the Theory of the Firm, *Journal of Law and Society*, 24(1): 124–151.

European Commission (2004) *Directive on Minimum Transparency Requirements for Listed Companies*, Brussels, European Commission.

Frentrop, P.M.L. (2003) *A History of Corporate Governance 1602–2002*, Brussels: Deminor.

Fried, V., Bruton, G. and Hisrich, R. (1998) Strategy and the Board of Directors in Venture Capital-backed Firms, *Journal of Business Venturing*, 13(6): 493–503.

Gabrielsson, J. (2007) Correlates of Board Empowerment in Small Companies, *Entrepreneurship Theory and Practice*, 31(5), September: 687–711.

Gorton, G. and Schmid, F. (1996) *Universal Banking and the Performance of German Corporations*, NBER Working Paper, 5453.

Harvey-Jones, J. (1998) *Making It Happen*, London: Collins.

Hoshi, T., Kashyap, A. and Scharfstein, D. (1991) Corporate Structure, Liquidity, and Investment: Evidence from Japanese Industrial Groups, *Quarterly Journal of Business and Economics*, 106(1): 33–60.

Hosking, D.M. (1996) Negotiated Order, in N. Nicholson (ed.), *Encyclopaedic Dictionary of Organisational Behaviour*, Oxford: Blackwell Business.

Hoskisson, R.E., Hitt, M.A., Johnson, R.A. and Grossman, W. (2002) Conflicting Voices: The Effects of Institutional Ownership Heterogeneity and Internal Governance on Corporate Innovation Strategies, *Academy of Management Journal*, 45: 697–716.

Huse, M. (2005) Accountability and Creating Accountability: A Framework for Exploring Behavioural Perspectives of Corporate Governance, *British Journal of Management*, 16(s1): S65–S79.

ICGN (2013) *ICGN Statement of Principles for Institutional Investor Responsibilities*, London: International Corporate Governance Network.

Jacoby, S. (2001) Corporate Governance in Comparative Perspective: Prospects for Convergence, *Comparative Labour Law and Policy Journal*, 22(1): 5–28.

Jacoby, S.M. (2002) Corporate Governance in Comparative Perspective: Prospects for Convergence, *Comparative Labor Law & Policy Journal*, 22(1): 5–28.

Jensen, M.C. (1986) Agency Costs of Free Cash Flow, Corporate Finance and Takeovers, *American Economic Review*, 76(2): 323–329.

La Porta, R., Lopez-de-Silanes, F. and Shleifer, Al. (1999) Corporate Ownership around the World, *Journal of Finance*, 54(2): 471–517.

Lazonick, W. (1992) Controlling the Market for Corporate Control: The Historical Significance of Managerial Capitalism, *Industrial and Corporate Change*, 1(3): 445–488.

McDonnell, B.H. (2002). Convergence in Corporate Governance – Possible, but Not Desirable. *Villanova Law Review*, 47(2): 341–386.

McNulty, T., Roberts, J. and Stiles, P. (2003) *Creating Accountability within the Boardroom: The Work of the Effective Non-Executive Director*, Research Report, Higgs Inquiry, London: Department of Trade and Industry.

OECD (2004) *Corporate Governance: A Survey of OECD Countries*, Paris: OECD.

OECD (2015a) OECD/G20 *Base Erosion and Profit Shifting Project Explanatory Statement*, 2015 Final Reports, OECD, www.oecd.org/tax/beps-explanatory-statement-2015.pdf

OECD (2015b) *G20/OECD Principles of Corporate Governance*, Paris: OECD.

OECD (2021) *Corporate Governance Factbook*, Paris: OECD https://www.oecd.org/corporate/corporategovernance-factbook.htm.

Piore, M.J. (2004) *Innovation, the Missing Dimension*, Cambridge, MA: Harvard University Press

Porter, M.E. (1992) Capital Disadvantage: America's Failing Capital Investment System, *Harvard Business Review*, 70(5): 65–82.

Pugliese, A. and Zattoni, A. (2012) Board's Contribution to Strategy and Innovation, in T. Clarke and D. Branson (eds.), *Sage Handbook of Corporate Governance* (pp. 217–232), London: Sage.

Pugliese, A., Bezemer, P.J., Zattoni, A., et al. (2009) Boards of Directors' Contribution to Strategy: A Literature Review and Research Agenda, *Corporate Governance: An International Review*, 17: 292–306.

Roe, M.J. (1994) *Strong Managers, Weak Owners: The Political Roots of American Corporate Finance*, Princeton, NJ: Princeton University Press.

Rybczynski, T. (1997) *The Recent Evolution of Financial Systems*, New York, St Martin's Press.

Sanders, W.M. and Carpenter, M.A. (1998) Internationalization and Firm Governance: The Roles of CEO Compensation, Top Team Composition and Board Structure, *Academy of Management Journal*, 14: 158–178.

Stiles, P. and Taylor, B. (2002) *Boards at Work: How Directors View Their Roles and Responsibilities*, Oxford: Oxford University Press.

Streeck, W. (2001) *The Transformation of Corporate Organization in Europe: An Overview*, Cologne: Max Planck Institute, MPIFG Working Paper, 01/8.

Sundaramurthy, C. and Lewis, M. (2003) Control and Collaboration: Paradoxes of Governance, *Academy of Management Review*, 28(3): 397–415.

Taggart, R.A. (1986) Have US Corporations Grown Financially Weak?, in B.M. Friedman (ed.), *Financing Corporate Capital Formation*, Chicago, IL: University of Chicago Press.

Tihanyi, L., Johnson, R.A., Hoskisson, R.E. and Hitt, M.A. (2003) Institutional Ownership Differences and International Diversification: The Effects of Boards of Directors and Technological Opportunity, *Academy of Management Journal*, 46: 195–211.

UK Code (2014) *The UK Corporate Governance Code*, London: The Financial Reporting Council Limited.

UNCTAD (2006) *Guidance on Good Practices in Corporate Governance Disclosure*, Geneva: UNEP.

US Congress (2002) *Sarbanes–Oxley Act*, Washington, DC: US Congress.

Vienot Report (1999) *Recommendations of the Committee on Corporate Governance*, Association Francaise Des Enterprises Privees AFEP, Mouvement Des Enterprises de France Medef.

Westphal, J.D. and Fredrickson, J.W. (2001) Who Directs Strategic Change? Director Experience, the Selection of New CEOs, and Change in Corporate Strategy, *Strategic Management Journal*, 22(12): 1113–1137.

Williamson, O.E. (1998) Corporate Finance and Corporate Governance, *Journal of Finance*, 63(3): 567–591.

Zahra, S.A. and Filatotchev, I. (2004) Governance of the Entrepreneurial Threshold Firm: A Knowledge-Based Perspective, *Journal of Management Studies*, 41(5): 885–897.

Zahra, S.A., Filatotchev, I. and Wright, M. (2009) How Do Threshold Firms Sustain Corporate Entrepreneurship? The Role of Boards and Absorptive Capacity, *Journal of Business Venturing*, 24: 248–260.

Zahra, S.A., Neubaum, D.O. and Huse, M. (2000) Entrepreneurship in Medium-Sized Companies: Exploring the Effects of Ownership and Governance Systems, *Journal of Management*, 26(5): 947–976.

3 Convergence and Divergence of International Corporate Governance Institutions

Introduction

This chapter examines the continuing diversity of corporate governance by critically analysing the impelling financial forces for convergence and the vitality of institutional differentiation. Convergence implies the increasing adoption by all governance systems throughout the world of a common set of institutions and practices, portrayed as an ideal rational-legal system, but invariably resting upon a belief in the virtue of market-based relationships, and the associated paradigms of the prevailing Anglo-American economic and legal orthodoxy, which insists the creation of shareholder value is the ultimate objective of corporate existence. By contrast, institutional differentiation approaches recognise the ongoing vitality of differentiation in the institutions, policies, and practices of corporate governance; how this reflects differences in culture, values, and conceptions of corporate purpose; and why this contributes to quality and variety in regional industries and products.

Competing theories of convergence and diversity are examined through the disciplinary perspectives of history and politics, law and regulation, culture, and institutional complementarities. A central thesis of the analysis is the increasing intensification of the financialisation of the global economy, which translates for corporations into an enveloping regime of maximising shareholder value as the primary objective. These financial pressures may have originated in the Anglo-American world and are manifest in the vast international scale and penetration of Anglo-American financial institutions; however, similar developments are becoming insistent in Europe, Asia-Pacific, and throughout the emerging economies. Yet diversified governance institutions confronted by these continuous pressures for international convergence have proved resilient and viable.

DOI: 10.4324/9780429294648-3

The conclusion of the analysis is that this differentiation is valuable since different governance systems are better at doing different things, as revealed in the relative strengths and weaknesses in governance, investment strategy, and product specialisation. In practice, simultaneously there may be a dual dynamic of convergence and divergence taking place, where corporations learn to live with some of the pressures of international financial markets yet value the differentiation of their regional cultures and institutions, while they strive to maintain and enhance the distinctiveness of their corporate objectives.

Indeed, a fatal flaw of the convergence thesis is the assumption that some uniform, homogenised, corporate governance system would in all circumstances prove superior both functionally and institutionally to the present diversified system. In fact, as a result of the differences in corporate governance structure and objectives, the different governance systems demonstrate unique strengths and weaknesses: they are good at doing different things, and they all have different problems to deal with (Clarke and Bostock 1994; Moerland 1995; Coombes and Watson 2000; Dore 2002; Clarke 2016; Clarke and Branson 2012). Anglo-American governance systems support a dynamic market orientation with fluid capital which can quickly chase market opportunities wherever they occur. This agility, ready availability of capital, intelligence, and speed have enabled the US to capitalise on fast-moving industries, including media, software, professional services, and finance in an industrial resurgence that temporarily reasserted US economic ascendancy.

The weakness of this system is the corollary of its strength: the inherent volatility, short-termism, and inadequate governance procedures that have often led to corporate disasters and have caused periodic financial crises (Clarke 2013). Adopting a different orientation European enterprise as typified by the German governance system has committed to long-term industrial strategies supported by stable capital investment and robust governance procedures that build enduring relationships with key stakeholders (Lane 2003; Cernat 2004). This was the foundation of the German economic miracle that carried the country forward as one of the leading exporters in the world of goods renowned for their exceptional quality and reliability including luxury automobiles and precision instruments.

Again, the weaknesses of this system are the corollary of its strengths: the depth of relationships leading to a lack of flexibility in pursuing new business opportunities in new industries and internationally. It should be noted that the German system of governance is typical of the coordinated market economies (Japan, Sweden, and

Germany) of northern Europe that have concentrated ownership and overall co-operative relations with employees compared to the mixed market Latin economies (France, Italy, and Spain) which also have concentrated ownership but more conflictual relations between employers and employees (Hancké et al. 2007; Hancké 2009; Goyer and Jung 2011).

In Asia, corporate governance systems are the most networked of all, with the firm at the centre of long and enduring economic relationships with investors, employees, suppliers, and customers (Claessens and Fan 2002). This insider approach has yielded the longest investment horizons of all and was, for example, the key to Japanese success in dominating overseas markets in the US and Europe with advanced electronic consumer goods, as well as in affordable quality automobiles. More recently, the capacity for investing in the long term has seen the entrance onto the world stage of impressive Chinese corporations such as the Industrial and Commercial Bank of China as the world's largest bank by assets, and Huawei as one of the world's leading telecommunications manufacturers. However just as the weak and secretive corporate governance practices of Japan ultimately led to the bursting of the Japanese bubble in the early 1990s, and to successive governance problems since, so too the apparently inexorable rise of a Chinese enterprise is threatened by covert governance and lack of transparency and accountability in finance.

A more realistic perspective than the convergence thesis is a more nuanced understanding that despite the financial and other market pressures towards convergence, there will continue to be considerable diversity in the forms of corporate governance developing around the world. Different traditions, values, and objectives will undoubtedly continue to produce different outcomes in governance, which will relate closely to the choices and preferences people exercise in engaging in business activity. If there is convergence of corporate governance, it could be to a variety of different forms, and it is likely there will be divergence away from the shareholder-oriented Anglo-American model, as there will be convergence towards it.

There is a growing realisation that shareholder value is a debilitating ideology which is undermining corporations with an oversimplification of complex business reality, weakening managers, corporations and economies, and ignoring the diversity of investment institutions and interests (Clarke 2014, 2015; Lazonick 2014). Moreover, the convergence "one-size-fits-all" approach studiously denies the essential entrepreneurship and creativity involved in business endeavour that will continuously give rise to innovative and dynamic forms of corporate governance as we are presently seeing in new forms of social enterprise, B-corporations, and other business ventures which, in turn, create and develop new complementary institutions.

A Universal Corporate Governance System?

In the contest between three resolutely different approaches to corporate governance in the Anglo-American, European and Asia-Pacific models, the question arises: is one system more robust than the others and will this system prevail and become universal? The answer to this question appeared straightforward in the 1990s. The US economy was ascendant, and the American market-based approach appeared the most dynamic and successful. Functional convergence towards the market-based system seemed to be occurring inexorably driven by forces such as:

*   Increasingly massive international financial flows which offered deep, liquid capital markets to countries and companies that could meet certain minimum international corporate governance standards.
*   Growing influence of the great regional stock exchanges, including the New York Stock Exchange (NYSE) and NASDAQ, London Stock Exchange, and Euronext – where the largest corporations in the world were listed regardless of their home country.
*   Developing activity of ever-expanding Anglo-American-based gargantuan institutional investors, advancing policies to balance their portfolios with increasing international investments if risk could be mitigated.
*   Expanding revenues and market capitalisation of multinational enterprises (often Anglo-American corporations, invariably listed on the NYSE even if European based), combined with a sustained wave of international mergers and acquisitions from which increasingly global companies were emerging.
*   Accelerating convergence towards international accounting standards; a worldwide governance movement towards more independent auditing standards, and rigorous corporate governance practices.

Together these forces have provoked one of the liveliest debates of the past two decades concerning the globalisation and convergence of corporate governance (Roe 2000, 2003; Branson 2001; Hansmann and Kraakman 2001; McCahery et al. 2002; McDonnell 2002; Aguilera and Jackson 2003; Gunter and van der Hoeven 2004; Lomborg 2004;

Hamilton and Quinlan 2005; Jesovar and Kirkpatrick 2005; Deeg and Jackson 2007; Jacoby 2007; Williams and Zumbansen 2011; Aguilera et al. 2012; Jackson and Deeg 2012; Jackson and Sorge 2012; Clarke 2014, 2016). As functional convergence proceeds in the way corporate access to finance and governance practices become universal, it is assumed that institutional convergence of legal and regulatory bodies and governance institutions will become identical. How high the stakes are in this debate is revealed by Gordon and Roe:

> Globalization affects the corporate governance reform agenda in two ways. First, it heightens anxiety over whether particular corporate governance systems confer competitive economic advantage. As trade barriers erode, the locally protected product marketplace disappears. A country's firms' performance is more easily measured against global standards. Poor performance shows up more quickly when a competitor takes away market share or innovates quickly. National decision makers must consider whether to protect locally favored corporate governance regimes if they regard the local regime as weakening local firms in product markets or capital markets. Concern about comparative economic performance induces concern about corporate governance. Globalization's second effect comes from capital markets' pressure on corporate governance. ... Despite a continuing bias in favor of home-country investing, the internationalization of capital markets has led to more cross-border investing. New stockholders enter, and they aren't always part of any local corporate governance consensus. They prefer a corporate governance regime they understand and often believe that reform will increase the value of their stock. Similarly, even local investors may make demands that upset a prior local consensus. The internationalization of capital markets means that investment flows may move against firms perceived to have suboptimal governance and thus to the disadvantage of the countries in which those firms are based.
>
> (2004: 2)

In the inevitable contest between the insider, relationship-based, stakeholder-oriented corporate governance system and the outsider, market-based, shareholder value-oriented system, it is often implied that the optimal model is the dispersed ownership with shareholder foci for achieving competitiveness and enhancing any economy in a globalised world. The OECD, World Bank, International Monetary Fund (IMF), Asian Development Bank, and other international agencies, while they have recognised the existence of different governance systems and suggested they would not wish to adopt a one-size-fits-all approach, have nonetheless consistently associated the *rules-based* outsider mode of corporate governance with greater efficiency and capacity to attract investment capital, and relegated the relationship-based insider mode to second-best, often with the implication that these systems may be irreparably flawed. The drive towards functional convergence was supported by the development of increasing numbers of international codes and standards of corporate governance.

The vast weight of scholarship, led by the financial economists, has reinforced these ideas to the point where they appeared unassailable at the height of the new economy boom in the US in the 1990s (which coincided with a long recession for both the leading exponents of the relationships-based system, Japan and Germany), supporting the view that an inevitable convergence towards the superior Anglo-American model of corporate governance was occurring. This all appeared as an integral part of the irresistible rise of globalisation and financialisation that was advancing through the regions of the world in the late 1990s and early 2000s, with apparently unstoppable force. Economies, cultures, and peoples increasingly were becoming integrated into global markets, media networks, and foreign ideologies in a way never before experienced. It seemed as if distinctive and valued regional patterns of corporative governance would be absorbed just as completely as other cultural institutions in the integrative and homogenising processes of globalisation. The increasing power of global capital markets, stock exchanges, institutional investors, and international regulation would overwhelm cultural and institutional differences in the approach to corporate governance.

Yet just as there are many countries that continue to value greatly the distinctions of their culture and institutions they would not wish to lose to any globalised world, people also believe there are unique attributes to the different corporate governance systems they have developed over time and are not convinced these should be sacrificed to some unquestioning acceptance that a universal system will inevitably be better. The field of comparative corporate governance has continued to develop, however, and a different and more complex picture of governance systems is now emerging. The objectives of corporate governance are more closely questioned; the qualities of the variety and relationships of different institutional structures are becoming more apparent; the capability and performance of the different systems more closely examined; and different potential outcomes of any convergence of governance systems realised.

While capital markets have acquired an apparently irresistible force in the world economy, it still appears that institutional complementarities at the national and regional levels represent immovable objects (Deeg and Jackson 2007; Jacoby 2007; Williams and Zumbansen 2011; Jackson and Deeg 2012; Clarke 2014, 2016). This is not to argue the immutability of institutions which, of course, are continuously engaged in complex processes of creation, development, and reinvention in the economic, social, and cultural contexts in which they exist. However, what is at issue is the causation and direction of these institutional changes. From the convergence perspective, they are a logical result of adopting the superior Anglo-American institutions of corporate governance and financial markets. From the perspective of those who respect and understand the reasons for institutional diversity and value the outcomes of this diversity, institutional change is a more autonomous process embedded within economies and societies, which may indeed have to negotiate some settlement with international market forces, but strive to do so while maintaining their own values.

An apparent third possibility to the two polar positions of convergence/institutional diversity is recognised by Coffee (2001, 2002) and Gilson (2000). Coffee (2002) distinguishes "functional convergence" (similarities in activities and objectives) from "formal convergence" (common legal rules and institutions) and contends that functional substitutes may provide alternative means to the same ends (e.g. a European company with weak investor protection and securities markets could list on the London or New York exchanges with rules that require greater disclosure of information, providing a framework of protections for minority shareholders not available in common law countries). Coffee argues that while the law matters, legal reforms follow rather than lead market changes. Gilson (2000:10) offers a more robust view of the force of functional convergence:

> Path dependency, however, is not the only force influencing the shape of corporate governance institutions. Existing institutions are subject to powerful environmental selection mechanisms. If existing institutions cannot compete with differently organized competitors, ultimately they will not survive. Path dependent formal characteristics of national governance institutions confront the discipline of the operative selection mechanisms that encourage functional convergence to the more efficient structure and, failing that, formal convergence as well.

This view from Columbia University Law School of the ascendancy of functional governance in Europe and elsewhere might have carried more weight if Coffee had not concluded his 2000 paper with a celebration of Germany's rapidly growing *Neuer Markt* as the "clearest example" of self-regulatory alternative functional governance creating a greater constituency for open and transparent markets. In fact, Germany's *Neuer Markt* launched as Europe's answer to the NASDAQ in 1997, collapsed with a precipitous decline in market value and numerous bankruptcies in 2003, leaving the question of how innovative German firms could enter the public equity markets unresolved (Burghof and Hunger 2003).

As von Kalckreuth and Silbermann (2010) state, this represented

> the spectacular rise and fall of the first and most important European market for hi-tech stocks. Given investors' frenzy, the Neuer Markt was a special kind of natural experiment. For some time, financing constraints were virtually non-existent, but as occurred, faulty valuation by stock markets may directly induce destructive corporate behaviour: slack, empire building, excessive risk-taking, and fraud.

While more viable illustrations of functional convergence could readily be found, it could be argued that this approach is largely another route to the convergence thesis rather than an alternative. Indeed functional convergence, since it is easier to achieve than institutional convergence, could prove a quicker route to shareholder value orientations.

Globalisation of Capital Markets

The convergence thesis is derived essentially from the globalisation thesis: that irresistible market forces are impelling the integration of economies and societies. Globalisation represents a profound reconfiguration of the world economy compared to earlier periods of internationalisation. "An international economy *links* distinct national markets: a global economy *fuses* national markets into a coherent whole" (Kobrin 2002: 7; Clarke and dela Rama 2006). A major driver of the globalisation phenomenon has proved the massive development of the financial markets, and their increasing influence upon every other aspect of the economy:

> Financial globalisation, that is the integration of more and more countries into the international financial system and the expansion of international markets for money, capital and foreign exchange, took off in the 1970s. From the 1980s on, the increase in cross-border holdings of assets outpaced the increase in international

trade, and financial integration accelerated once more in the 1990s ... The past decade has also seen widespread improvements in macroeconomic and structural policies that may to some extent be linked to a disciplining effect of financial integration. Moreover, there is evidence that financial linkages have strengthened the transmission of cyclical impulses and shocks among industrial countries. Financial globalisation is also likely to have helped the build-up of significant global current account imbalances. Finally, a great deal of the public and academic discussion has focussed on the series of financial crises in the 1990s, which has highlighted the potential effects of capital account liberalisation on the volatility of growth and consumption.

(European Commission 2005: 19)

The complex explanation for this massive *financialisation* of the world economy is pieced together by Ronald Dore thus:

- Financial services take up an ever-larger share of advertising, economic activity, and highly skilled manpower.
- Banks respond to the decline in loan business with a shift to earning fees for financial and investment services and own account trading.
- Shareholder value is preached as the sole legitimate objective and aspiration of corporations and executives.
- Insistent and demanding calls for "level playing fields" from the World Trade Organization and Bank of International Settlements (BIS), with pressures for the further liberalisation of financial markets, and greater international competition forcing international financial institutions, and other corporations to work within the same parameters (Dore 2000: 4–6).

What is resulting from this insistent impulse of the increasingly dominant financial institutions are economies (and corporations) becoming dependent upon financial markets:

Global integration and economic performance has been fostered by a new dynamic in financial markets, which both mirrors and amplifies the effects of foreign direct investment and trade driven integration. The economic performance of countries across the world is increasingly supported by – and dependent on – international capital flows, which have built on a process of progressive liberalisation and advances in technology since the 1980s.

(European Commission 2005: 8)

Financial innovations and financial cycles have periodically impacted substantially economies and societies, most notably in the recent global financial crisis (Clarke 2010a; Rajan 2010). However, the new global era of financialisation is qualitatively different from earlier regimes. Global finance is now typified by a more international, integrated, and intensive mode of accumulation; a new business imperative of the maximisation of shareholder value; and a remarkable capacity to become an intermediary in every aspect of daily life (van der Zwan 2013). Hence, finance as a phenomenon today is more universal, aggressive, and pervasive than ever before (Epstein 2005; Krippner 2005, 2012; Dore 2008; Davis 2009; de Zwan 2013).

These financial pressures are translated into the operations of corporations through the enveloping regime of maximising shareholder value as the primary objective. Agency theory has provided the rationale for this project, prioritising shareholders above all other participants in the corporation, and focusing corporate managers on the release of shareholder value incentivised by their own stock options. In turn, this leads to an obsessive emphasis on financial performance measures, with increasingly short-term business horizons (Lazonick 2012, 2014; Clarke 2013).

The Growth of International Equity Markets

A vital dimension of the increasing financialisation of the world economy is the growth of capital markets, and especially the vast growth of equity markets, where volatility has been experienced at its furthest extremities. What this demonstrates is the overwhelming predominance of Anglo-American institutions and activity in the world equity markets, and how to a great extent these markets reflect largely Anglo-American interests, as the rest of the world depends more on other sources of corporate finance. This pre-eminence of equity markets is a very recent phenomenon.

Historically, the primary way most businesses throughout the world (including in the Anglo-American region) have financed the growth of their companies is internally through retained earnings. In most parts of the world until recently, this was a far more dependable source of capital rather than relying on equity markets. Equity finance has proved useful at the time of public listing when entrepreneurs and venture capitalists cash in their original investment, as a means of acquiring other companies, or providing rewards for executives through stock options. Equity finance is used much less frequently during restructuring or to finance new product or project development (Lazonick 1992:

457). In Europe and the Asia-Pacific, however, this capital was in the past provided by majority shareholders, banks, or other related companies (to the extent it was needed by companies committed to organic growth rather than through acquisition, and where executives traditionally were content with more modest personal material rewards than their American counterparts).

The euphoria of the US equity markets did reach across the Atlantic with a flurry of new listings, which formed part of a sustained growth in the market capitalisation of European stock exchanges as a percentage of gross domestic product (GDP). A keen attraction of equity markets for ambitious companies is the possibility of using shares in equity swaps as a means of taking over other companies thus fuelling the take-over markets of Europe. This substantial development of the equity markets of France, the Netherlands, Germany, Spain, Belgium, and other countries began to influence the corporate landscape of Europe, and was further propelled by the formation of Euronext, and the subsequent merger with the NYSE.

Indeed as the regulatory implications of Sarbanes Oxley emerged in the US from 2003 onwards, the market for initial public offerings (IPOs) moved emphatically towards London, Hong Kong, and other exchanges. Concerned about the impact of Sarbanes Oxley on the US economy a group of authorities formed the Committee on Capital Markets Regulation that highlighted the damage being caused to what for many years was recognised as "the largest, most liquid, and most competitive public equity capital markets in the world" (CCMR 2006: ix). Though the total share of the US in the global stock market activity remained at 50 per cent in 2005, the IPO activity had collapsed. From attracting 48 per cent of global IPOs in the late 1990s, the US share dropped to 6 per cent in 2005, when 24 of the 25 largest IPOs were in other countries (CCMR 2006: 2). The more relaxed regulatory environment of the UK and other jurisdictions clearly for a time at least proved attractive in an ongoing process of international regulatory arbitrage.

This greater vibrancy in European markets partly explains the NYSE's interest in merging with Euronext, and the NASDAQ's long but failed courtship with the London Stock Exchange. Any such mergers represent a further US bridgehead into the equity markets of Europe, rather than the converse. Along with the growth in market capitalisation in European exchanges occurred a gradual increase also in trading value. It appears that contemporary equity markets inevitably will be associated with high levels of trading activity, as a growing proportion of trading is algorithmic high-frequency and computer-generated. Following the global financial crisis, regulatory intervention in finance was perceived to be more robust in Europe and the UK, and less so in the US (with the slow pace of the introduction of the monumental Dodd-Frank Act). In this context, the attractions of the NYSE and NASDAQ returned, and by 2014 reached once again the levels of IPO financing in the dot.com 1990s era, far exceeding the amounts raised in the London and Hong Kong markets combined (*Financial Times*, 29 September 2014).

The important role of equity markets in fostering further international financial integration was recognised by the European Commission (2005): "Globally, portfolio investment is the largest asset category held cross-border; global portfolios (equity and debt securities) amounted to 19 trillion US dollar at the end of 2003 (IMF CPIS, preliminary data)." As equity markets come to play a more powerful role in corporate life in Europe, Japan, and other parts of the world, a set of assumptions and practices are also disseminated which may confront long-standing values and ideals in the economies and societies concerned. Specifically, the ascendancy of shareholder value as the single legitimate objective of corporations and their executives, usually accompanies increasing dependence upon equity markets. Dore cites a Goldman Sachs study of manufacturing value added in the US, Germany, and Europe in general, which concluded that:

> The share of gross value added going to wages and salaries has declined on trend in the US since the early 1980s. In fact, for the US, this appears to be an extension of a trend that has been in place since the early 1970s ... We believe that the pressures of competition for the returns on capital available in the emerging economies have forced US industry to produce higher returns on equity capital and that their response to this has been to reserve an increasingly large share of output for the owners of capital.
>
> (Young 1997)

This insistent pressure to drive increases in capital's returns at the expense of labour inherent in Anglo-American conceptions of the nature of equity finance is roundly condemned by Dore as the negation of essential values previously considered central to economic good in both Europe and Japan:

> Multiple voices are urging Japanese managers to go in the same direction. The transformation on the agenda may be variously described – from employee sovereignty to shareholder sovereignty:

from the employee-favouring firm to the shareholder-favouring firm; from pseudo-capitalism to genuine capitalism. They all mean the same thing: the transformation of firms run primarily for the benefits of their employees into firms run primarily, even exclusively, for the benefit of their shareholders ... It means an economy centred on the stock market as the measure of corporate success and on the stock market index as a measure of national well-being, as opposed to an economy which has other, better, more pluralistic criteria of human welfare for measuring progress towards the good society.

(2000: 9–10)

The euphoric enthusiasm for the power of equity markets was severely dented by the Enron/WorldCom series of corporate collapses in the US. With about seven trillion dollars wiped off the NYSE in 2001/2002, and the executives of many leading corporations facing criminal prosecution. Yet the recovery in equity markets came sooner and more robustly than expected. However, part of the price of restoring confidence to the markets was the hasty passage of the Sarbanes Oxley legislation and increased regulation of corporate governance.

Sarbanes-Oxley apparently did little to curb the animal spirits of some fringes of the US financial institutions that ultimately impacted on the world economy. The subprime mortgage crisis, and the elaborate financial instruments developed to pass on risk by investment banks, that caused a prolonged implosion of financial institutions in the global financial crisis of 2007/2008 was an indication of the dangers presented by the increasing financialisation of economic activity, and the hazardous context for corporate governance in market-oriented economies (Clarke 2010a). Nonetheless, despite the strenuous intervention of the G20, Financial Stability Board internationally and the Dodd-Frank legislation in the US intended to restrain the most dangerous impulses of financial institutions, the strength and vigour of capital markets seem destined to continue to advance globally without adequate regulation or oversight (Clarke and Klettner 2011; Avgouleas 2013).

While each of the regional systems of finance and corporate governance remains in the post-financial crisis period weakened and to a degree disoriented, the substance and rhythm of institutional varieties continues: in Germany, there remains an incomplete form of market liberalisation, and resilient elements of the social market economy (Jackson and Sorge, 2012); in France, while the neo-liberal reforms have undermined social alliances and the pressures for institutional change increase, social commitments continue (Amable et al. 2012);

and in Japan, the incursions of hedge funds and private equity with a growing proportion of overseas ownership of Japanese corporations have not deflected Japanese executives from maintaining more inclusive conceptions in their definition of corporate purpose (Seki and Clarke 2014).

Convergence and Diversity of Corporate Governance

Despite the recurrent crises originating in Anglo-American finance and governance in this period, and in the background, the continuing reverberations of the global financial crisis, the confidence the market-based system was the only way forward has continued almost undaunted in government and business circles, certainly in the Anglo-American world (Clarke 2010a). Underlying the resurging energy of advancing equity markets and the proliferating corporate governance guidelines and policy documents appearing in such profusion over the past two decades is an implicit but confident sense that an optimal corporate governance model is indeed emerging:

> An optimal model with dispersed ownership and shareholder foci ... The OECD and World Bank promote corporate governance reform ... Influenced by financial economists and are generally promoting market capitalism with a *law matters* approach, although for political reasons, they do not advocate too strongly market capitalism and allow for other corporate governance systems (i.e. concentrated ownership).
>
> (Pinto 2005, 26–27)

Other authorities are less diplomatic in announcing the superiority of the Anglo-American approach that other systems must inevitably converge towards. Two US eminent law school professors Hansmann and Kraakman in an article prophetically entitled "The End of History for Corporate Law" led the charge of the convergence determinists:

> Despite very real differences in the corporate systems, the deeper tendency is towards convergence, as it has been since the nineteenth century. The core legal features of the corporate form were already well established in advanced jurisdictions one hundred years ago, at the turn of the twentieth century. Although there remained considerable room for variation in governance practices and in the fine structure of corporate law throughout the twentieth century, the pressures for further convergence are now rapidly

growing. Chief among these pressures is the recent dominance of a shareholder-centred ideology of corporate law among the business, government and legal entities in key commercial jurisdictions. There is no longer any serious competitor to the view that corporate law should principally strive to increase long-term shareholder value. This emergent consensus has already profoundly affected corporate governance practices throughout the world. It is only a matter of time before its influence is felt in the reform of corporate law as well.

(2001:1)

The irony of this profoundly ideological claim (the most recent in a long historical lineage of similar appeals) is that it attempts to enforce the consensus it claims exists, by crowding out any possibility of alternatives. This is not an isolated example, but the dominant approach of much legal and financial discussion in the US, where as McDonnell insists the prevailing view is:

The American system works better and that the other countries are in the process of converging to the American system. Though there is some dissent from this position, the main debate has been over why countries outside the United States have persisted for so long in their benighted systems and what form their convergence to the American way will take. The scholarly discussion has converged too quickly on the convergence answer.

(2002: 2)

It is worth asking by what standards or criteria a system of corporate governance may be defined as "optimal." Where a definition is offered in the convergence literature for an optimal corporate governance system it invariably relates to accountability to shareholders, and often to maximising shareholder value which became an increasingly insistent ideology in Anglo-American analyses of corporate purpose. The narrow financial metrics relating to maximising shareholder value often are presented as the only valid measures of an optimal corporate governance system, when there are deeper and wider measures that could be employed in the estimation of business performance.

Business success might be measured in longevity, scale, revenue, sales, employment, product quality, customer satisfaction, or many other measures that might be found relevant in different societies at different times. Certainly, the measures of business success employed in Europe and Asia are quite different from the Anglo-Saxon world and would embrace wider stakeholder interests. Most economic analyses simply substitute "efficient" for optimal, but McDonnell offers three relevant values:

a efficiency
b equity
c participation

In considering efficiency, there is the question of how well the governance system solves agency problems; how well the system facilitates large-scale coordination problems; how well the systems encourage long-term innovation; and how they impose different levels of risk on the participants. Distributional equity is another important value, but again is difficult to measure. For many, distributional equity suggests increased prosperity should provide for an increased equality of income and wealth, but others find this less compelling. In some instances, equity may conflict with efficiency: it could be argued that the US system is more efficient but inevitably results in greater inequality. Alternatively, equity may be associated with more collaborative creativity. Finally, there is the value of participation, both in terms of any contribution this may make to the success of the enterprise and as an end in itself in enhancing the ability and self-esteem of people. Corporate governance systems affect the level of participation in decision-making very directly, whether encouraging or disallowing active participation in enterprise decision-making (McDonnell 2002: 4).

Arguably, each of these values is of great importance, and the precise balance between them is part of the choice of what kind of corporate governance system is adopted. Yet there appears increasingly less opportunity to exercise this choice:

> The universe of theoretical possibilities is much richer than a dominant strand of the literature suggests, and we are currently far short of the sort of empirical evidence that might help us sort out these possibilities. Most commentators have focused on efficiency to the exclusion of other values. Moreover, even if convergence occurs, there is a possibility that we will not converge on the best system. Even if we converge to the current best system, convergence still may not be desirable.
>
> (McDonnell 2002: 2)

History and Politics

In the past, these critical political choices on which system of governance provides the most value in terms of efficiency, equity and participation have been made and defended. Mark Roe's (1994, 2003) path dependence thesis rests on how political forces in America, anxious about the influence of concentrated financial or industrial monopolies, resisted any effort at a concentration of ownership or ownership through financial institutions, resulting in dispersed ownership. In contrast, European social democracy has tended to favour other stakeholder interests, particularly labour, as a system that promotes welfare among all citizens and attempts to prevent wide disparities. In turn, this can be viewed as a reaction to the historical rise of fascism and communism (Pinto 2005: 22). Fligstein and Freeland (1995) adopt a similar historical view that the form of governance is a result of wider political and institutional developments:

i   the timing of entry into industrialisation and the institutionalisation of that process;
ii   the role of states in regulating property rights and the rules of competition between firms; and
iii   the social organisation of national elites (1995: 21).

In this way, characteristic institutions of the US economy can be traced back to distinctive political and regulatory intervention, resulting, for example, in historically distributed banks, diversified companies, and the dominance of the diversified (M-form) corporations. In contrast, in Europe and Japan, the regulatory environment encouraged a very different approach:

> Regulatory policy in the United States had the unintended consequence of pushing U.S. companies in the direction of unrelated diversification, whereas in Germany and Japan it continued on a pre-war trajectory of discouraging mergers in favour of cartels and of promoting corporate growth through internal expansion rather than acquisitions. In other words, modern regulatory policy in the U.S. produced corporations who relied on markets to acquire ideas and talent, whereas in Germany and Japan it produced corporations whose primary emphasis was on production and on the internal generation of ideas through development of human capital and organizational learning. The implications for corporate governance are straightforward: corporations favour shareholders in the U.S. so as to obtain capital for diversification and acquisitions; they favour managers and employees in the Germany and Japan so as to create internal organizational competencies.
>
> (Jacoby 2001: 8)

A very different reading of these events is offered by Rajan and Zingales (2003), who argue that widely dispersed shareholders is related to the development of liquid securities markets and the openness to outside investments, while it was not social democracy but protectionism that kept European and Japanese markets closed from the competition with concentrated ownership. As financial economists, they favour the globalisation route to open market-based competition, which they see as the way to unsettling local elites, achieving dispersed ownership, raising capital, and improving corporate governance.

Law and Regulation

Following a different line of analysis, the substantial empirical evidence of La Porta et al. (1998, 1999, 2000, 2002) concerning countries with dispersed and concentrated ownership demonstrating differences in the legal protection of shareholders was very influential. Law and regulation may impede or promote convergence or divergence. In many countries without adequate laws guaranteeing dispersed shareholder rights, the only alternative appeared to maintain control through concentrated ownership. This led to the conclusion that the law determined the ownership structure and system of corporate finance and governance. Jurisdictions where the law was more protective encouraged the emergence of more dispersed ownership (Pinto 2005: 19).

Coffee (2001) extends the La Porta et al.'s acceptance that in the common law system, there was greater flexibility of response to new developments offering better protection to shareholders, to the argument that the critical role of the decentralised character of common law institutions was to facilitate the rise of both private and semi-private self-regulatory bodies in the US and the UK. In contrast, in civil law systems, the state maintained a restrictive monopoly over law-making institutions (e.g. in the early intrusion of the French government into the affairs of the Paris Bourse involving the Ministry of Finance approving all new listings). Coffee concludes that it was market institutions that demanded legal protection rather than the other way around:

> The cause and effect sequence posited by the La Porta et al thesis may in effect read history backwards. They argue that strong markets require strong mandatory rules as a precondition. Although there is little evidence that strong legal rules encouraged the development of either the New York or London Stock Exchanges (and there is at least some evidence that strong legal rules hindered the growth of the Paris Bourse), the reverse does seem to be

true: strong markets do create a demand for stronger legal rules. Both in the U.S. and the U.K., as liquid securities markets developed and dispersed ownership became prevalent, a new political constituency developed that desired legal rules capable of filling in the inevitable enforcement gaps that self-regulation left. Both the federal securities laws passed in the 1930s in the U.S. and the Company Act amendments adopted in the late 1940s in the U.K. were a response to this demand (and both were passed by essentially "social democratic" administrations seeking to protect public securities markets). Eventually, as markets have matured across Europe, similar forces have led to the similar creation of European parallels to the SEC. In each case, law appears to be responding to changes in the market, not consciously leading it.

(Coffee 2001: 6)

Culture – Deep Causation

In the search for explanations, some have attempted a philosophical approach including Fukuyama (1996) who conceives of business organisations as the product of trust, and the different governance systems as built of different forms of trust relations. Regarding the social foundations and development of ownership structures and the law, other writers have examined the correlations between law and culture. Licht (2001) examines the relevance of national culture to corporate governance and securities regulation and explores the relationship between different cultural types and the law:

> A nation's culture can be perceived as the mother of all path dependencies. Figuratively, it means that a nation's culture might be more persistent than other factors believed to induce path dependence. Substantively, a nation's unique set of cultural values might indeed affect – in a chain of causality – the development of that nation's laws in general and its corporate governance system in particular.

(2001: 149)

In working towards a cross-cultural theory of corporate governance systems, Licht (2001) demonstrates that corporate governance laws exhibit systematic cultural characteristics.

A comparison between a taxonomy of corporate governance regimes according to legal families ("the legal approach") and a classification of countries according to their shared cultural values demonstrates that the legal approach provides only a partial, if not misleading, depiction of the universe of corporate governance regimes. Dividing shareholder protection regimes according to groups of culturally similar nations is informative. The evidence corroborates the uniqueness of common law origin regimes in better protecting minority shareholders. However, statutes in the English-speaking cultural region offer levels of protection to creditors similar to the laws in the Western European or Latin American regions. Our findings cast doubt on the alleged supremacy of common law regimes in protecting creditors and, therefore, investors in general. Finally, we find that analyses of corporate governance laws in Far Eastern countries, a distinct cultural region, would benefit from combining an approach that draws on cultural value dimensions and one that draws on legal families (Licht 2001: 32).

Licht concludes that corporations are embedded within larger socio-cultural settings in which they are incorporated and operate. Cultural values are influential in determining the types of legal regimes perceived and accepted as legitimate in any country and serve as a guide to legislators. Hence, cultural values may impede legal reforms that conflict with them and the naiveté underlying quick-fix suggestions for corporate law reform (2001: 33–34). Culture also influences what are perceived as the maximands of corporate governance – for example, in the debate over stockholders versus stakeholders interests as the ultimate objective of the corporation: "The corporate governance problem therefore is not one of maximising over a single factor (the maximand). Rather, it calls for optimizing over several factors simultaneously" (Licht 2003: 5). Berglöf and von Thadden (1999) suggest the economic approach to corporate governance should be generalised to a model of multilateral interactions among a number of different stakeholders. They argue that though protection of shareholder interests may be important, it may not be sufficient for sustainable development, particularly in transitional economies. Licht concludes:

> Every theory of corporate governance is at heart a theory of power. In this view, the corporation is a nexus of power relationships more than a nexus of contracts. The corporate setting is rife with agency relationships in which certain parties have the ability (power) unilaterally to affect the interests of other parties notwithstanding pre-existing contractual arrangements. In the present context, corporate fiduciaries are entrusted with the power to weigh and prefer the interests of certain constituencies to the interests of others (beyond their own self-interest). Given the current limitations of economic theory, progress in the analysis of the

maximands of corporate governance may be achieved by drawing on additional sources of knowledge.

(Licht 2003: 6)

Institutional Complementarities

A further development of the path dependence thesis is the emphasis on the interdependence of economic and social institutions: "Corporate governance consists not simply of *elements* but of *systems* ... Transplanting some of the formal elements without regard for the institutional complements may lead to serious problems later, and these problems may impede, or reverse, convergence" (Gordon and Roe 2004: 6). Optimal corporate governance mechanisms are contextual and may vary by industries and activities. Identifying what constitutes good corporate governance practice is complex and cannot be templated into a single form. One needs to identify the strengths and weaknesses in the system but also the underlying conditions which the system is dependent upon (Maher and Andersson 2000; Pinto 2005: 31). The institutions that compose the system of corporate governance and complement each other consist not just of the law, finance, and ownership structure.

Complementarities may extend to such things as labour relations and managerial incentive systems. In Germany and Japan, the corporations' long-term relations with banks, customers, and suppliers traditionally facilitate long-term commitments to employees. The commitment to permanency promotes extensive firm-specific training, which contributes to flexible specialisation in the production of high-quality goods. In contrast, in the US, employer training investments are lower than in Japan and Germany, employees are more mobile, and there is less firm-specific skill development. Similarly, in the US, fluid managerial labour markets make it easier for ousted managers to find new jobs after a hostile takeover. In contrast, in Japan, management talent is carefully evaluated over a long period of time through career employment and managerial promotion systems. Jacoby contends:

> It is difficult to disentangle the exogenous initial conditions that established a path from the *ex post* adaptations ... What's most likely to be the case is that capital markets, labour markets, legal regulations, and corporate norms co-evolved from a set of initial conditions.
>
> (2001: 17)

He continues with a warning to those who might wish to randomly transplant particular institutional practices into other countries:

Given institutional complementarities and path dependence, it's difficult for one country to borrow a particular practice and expect it to perform similarly when transplanted to a different context ... Were the Japanese or Germans to adopt a U.S.-style corporate governance approach that relies on takeovers to mitigate agency problems, it would prove highly disruptive of managerial incentive and selection systems presently in place. Hostile takeovers also would be disruptive of relations with suppliers and key customers, a substantial portion of which exist on a long term basis. In Germany and, especially, in Japan, there is less vertical integration of industrial companies than in the United States or the United Kingdom. Rather than rely primarily on arms-length contracts to protect suppliers and purchasers from opportunism, there is heavy use of relational contracting based on personal ties, trust, and reputation. Personal ties are supported by lifetime employment; the business relations are buttressed by cross-share holding. In short, imitation across path-dependent systems is inhibited by the cost of having to change a host of complementary practices that make an institution effective in a particular national system.

(Jacoby 2001: 18)

Another way of understanding this Jacoby suggests is through the concept of multiple equilibria, which leads to the conclusion there is no best way of designing institutions to support stability and growth in advanced industrial countries:

Multiple equilibria can arise and persist due to path dependence, institutional complementarities, bounded rationality, and comparative advantage. Sometimes multiple equilibria involve functionally similar but operationally distinctive institutions, such as the use of big firms as incubators in Japan versus the U.S. approach of incubation via start-ups and venture capital. Other times different institutions create qualitatively different outcomes. That is, a set of institutions, including those of corporate governance, may be better at facilitating certain kinds of business strategies and not others. Companies – and the countries in which they are embedded –can then secure international markets by specializing in those advantageous business strategies because foreign competitors will have difficulty imitating them. For example, the emphasis on specific human capital in German and Japan is supportive of production based technological learning, incremental innovation, and high quality production, all areas in which those

economies have specialized. By contrast, the U.S. emphasis on resource mobility and on high short-term rewards directs resources
to big-bang technological breakthroughs. In short, there are substantial gains to be reaped from sustaining institutional diversity
and competing internationally on that basis.

(Jacoby 2001: 25)

The discussion of corporate governance is often framed in static efficiency terms, Jacoby contends, as if it was possible to measure the
comparative performance of national governance institutions in a
static framework. This is inadequate for understanding the dynamic
properties of governance systems, especially concerning innovation
and long-term growth:

When there are multiple equilibria and bounded rationality regarding what constitutes an institutional optimum, we are operating in the world of the second best. In that world, there is no reason
to believe that revamping a governance system will necessarily
move an economy closer to an economic optimum. The economic
case for the superiority of Anglo-American governance – and of
the Anglo-American version of "free markets" as we know them,
as opposed to a theoretical ideal – is actually rather weak.

(Jacoby 2001: 27)

Integrated together the competing theories of convergence and diversity propounded in the disciplinary perspectives of history and politics,
law and regulation, culture, and institutional complementarities offer a
more nuanced prognosis of the future trends in corporate governance
than crudely deterministic theories of governance convergence suggest.
History and politics remind us of the relation of distinctive institutional
developments to the timing of industrialisation, the relative autonomy of
states in regulating property and competition, and the significance of the
structure and distribution of power and elites. Law and regulation im-
press upon us the significance of the distinctiveness of common and civil
law approaches, and how these respond to the maturing markets. Cultural approaches perceive the social foundations and distinctive values
that inform different regimes of governance. Finally, the institutional
complementarities approach identifies the interdependence of economic
and social institutions that create complex systems of governance. These
dynamic multiple equilibria of governance systems are unique, and
whilst they might exhibit some degree of functional similarity, they are
based on profoundly distinctive experiences, values, and objectives.

Different Governance Systems Are Better at Doing Different Things

For Hansmann and Kraakman, convergence of corporate governance systems towards the shareholder-oriented model is not only desirable and inevitable, it has already happened. They boldly confirm:

> The triumph of the shareholder-oriented model of the corporation over its principal competitors is now assured, even if it was problematic as recently as twenty-five years ago. Logic alone did not establish the superiority of this standard model or of the prescriptive rules that it implies, which establish a strong corporate management with duties to serve the interests of shareholders alone, as well as strong minority shareholder protections. Rather, the standard model earned its position as the dominant model of the large corporation the hard way, by out-competing during the post-World War II period the three alternative models of corporate governance: the managerialist model, the labour-oriented model, and the state-oriented model.
>
> (2001: 16)

For Hansmann and Kraakman, alternative systems are not viable competitively, only the lack of product market competition has kept them alive, and as global competitive pressures increase, any continuing viability of alternative models will be eliminated, encouraging the ideological and political consensus in favour of the shareholder model.

Hansmann and Kraakman dismiss the three rivals they set up for the victorious shareholder model. The managerialist model is associated with the US in the 1950s and 1960s, when it was thought professional managers could serve as disinterested technocratic fiduciaries who would guide the business corporation in the interests of the general public. According to Hansmann and Kraakman, this model of social benevolence collapsed into self-serving managerialism, with significant resource misallocation, imperilling the competitiveness of the model and accounting for its replacement by the shareholder-driven model in the US (Gordon and Roe 2004).

The labour-oriented model exemplified by German co-determination, but manifest in many other countries, possesses governance structures amplifying the representation of labour, which Hansmann and Kraakman claim are inefficient because of the heterogeneity of interests among employees themselves, and between employees and shareholders. Firms with this inherent competition of interests would inevitably lose out in product market competition. Finally, the state-oriented model associated with France or Germany entails a large state role in corporate affairs through ownership or state bureaucratic engagement with firm managers, allowing elite guidance of private enterprise in the public interest. Hansmann and Kraakman argue this corporatist model has been discredited because of the poor performance of socialist economies (Gordon and Roe 2004).

At the height of the NASDAQ boom when Hansmann and Kraakman wrote their visionary article, it might have appeared that the shareholder model in its US manifestation was certainly globally hegemonic in all of its manifestations. However, the post-global financial crisis world is less easily convinced of the inevitable and universal superiority of the US model of governance, and Hansmann and Kraakman may have written off the prospects of Japan and Europe a little too presumptuously, the best that could be salvaged from their overconfident thesis. The Anglo-American system might be better at doing some things which require the ready deployment of large amounts of liquid capital such as in high-tech innovation and global financial services. But the other governance systems have their own dynamism and valuable capabilities such as exhibited in German precision engineering, Japanese consumer electronics, French luxury goods, or Italian design. Essentially, it seems that the different corporate governance systems may be better at doing different things, and with different outcomes for the economy and society (Table 3.1).

The continuing diversity in Anglo-American, Germanic, Latin, and Japanese corporate governance systems is outlined in Table 3.1, indicating different orientations, concept of the firm, board structures, main stakeholders, the importance of stock and bond markets, the market for corporate control, ownership concentration, executive compensation, investment horizons, and the resulting corporate strengths and weaknesses that influence the types of products and services that are specialised in. The differences highlighted demonstrate that despite insistent pressures towards institutional and functional convergence, there remains a variety and distinctiveness in the regional approaches to corporate governance and strategy, which relates closely to their respective business strengths and weaknesses. There is a dynamism and vitality to this specialisation which continues to drive the distinctiveness and quality of the industries and products of these regions, despite the international financial, global value chain and functional pressures not only towards convergence but also towards bland homogeneity in global industries, products, and services.

Table 3.1 The Continuing Diversity of Corporate Governance Systems

Feature	Anglo-Saxon	Germanic	Latin	Japanese
Orientation	Market-oriented (an active external market for corporate control)	Market-oriented (relatively oligarchic, influenced by networks of shareholders, families and banks)	Network-oriented	Network-oriented
Representative countries	The US, the UK, Canada, Australia, New Zealand	Germany, the Netherlands, Switzerland, Sweden, Austria, Denmark, Norway, Finland	France, Italy, Spain, Belgium, Brazil, Argentina	Japan
Prevailing concept of the firm	Instrumental (as a means for creative shareholder value)	Institutional (autonomous economic units coming out of a coalition of shareholders, corporate managers, suppliers of goods and debts, and customers)	Institutional	Institutional
The Board system	One-tier (governance with one level of directors, making no distinction but executives and non-executives)	Two-tier (executive and supervisory board, the latter monitoring, appointing or dismissing managers; large shareholders on the Board and high pressure from banks)	Optional (France) in general one-tier	Board of directors, offices of representative directors, of auditors, de facto one-tier
Main stakeholders to exert influence on managerial decision-making	Shareholders	Industrial banks (mainly in Germany; in general, oligarchic group inclusive of employees' representatives)	Financial holdings, the government, families, in general oligarchic groups	City banks, other financial institutions, employees in general oligarchic groups

(Continued)

Feature	*Anglo-Saxon*	*Germanic*	*Latin*	*Japanese*
Importance of stock and bond markets	High (requiring continued action and performance)	Moderate or high (legal and regulatory bias against non-bank finance)	Moderate or poor	High (legal and regulatory bias against non-bank finance)
Is there a market for corporate control?	Yes	No	No	No
Ownership concentration	Low	Moderate or high (very high in Germany)	High	Low or moderate
Compensation based on performance	High	Low	Moderate	Low
Time horizon of economic relationships	Short-termism (management and governance myopia)	Long-termism	Long-termism	Long-termism
Strengths	Dynamic market orientation, fluid capital, internationalisation extensive	Long-term industrial strategy, very stable capital, robust governance procedures	Creative, aesthetic, flexible, continuity in skill development	Very long-term industrial strategy, stable capital, major overseas investment
Weaknesses	Volatile, short-termism, inadequate	Internationalisation more difficult, lack of flexibility, inadequate investment for new industries	Weak governance, majority control, little transparency	Financial speculation, secretive governance procedures, weak accountability.
Products	Financial services, software, high technology, media	Precision engineering, high-quality automobiles, high-quality manufacturing	Fashion goods, clothes, shoes, interior design goods	Automobiles and motorcycles, consumer electronics

Source: Adapted from Keenan and Aggestam (2001), Clarke and Bostock (1994).

As Douglas Branson concludes regarding the globalisation and convergence debate,

> seldom will one see scholarship and advocacy that is as culturally and economically insensitive, and condescending, as is the global convergence advocacy scholarship that the elites in United States academy have been throwing over the transom. Those elites have oversold an idea that has little grounding in true global reality.
>
> (2001: 276)

Bebchuk and Roe's (1999) view still holds that neither shareholder primacy nor dispersed ownership will easily converge. Path dependence has evolved established structures not easily transformed and complimentary institutions make it more difficult to do so. "Thus keeping existing systems may in fact be an efficient result. This lack of convergence allows for diversity and suggests that globalisation will not easily change the models" (Pinto 2005: 29).

A more realistic global perspective than the convergence thesis is that there will continue to be considerable diversity both in the forms of corporate governance around the world. Different traditions, values, and objectives will undoubtedly continue to produce different outcomes in governance, which will relate closely to the choices and preferences people exercise in engaging in business activity. If there is convergence of corporate governance, it could be to a variety of different forms, and it is likely there will be divergence away from the shareholder-oriented Anglo-American model, as there will be a convergence towards it. There is a growing realisation that shareholder value is a debilitating ideology which is undermining corporations with an over-simplification of complex business reality; weakening managers, corporations, and economies; and ignoring the diversity of investment institutions and interests (Clarke 2014; Lazonick 2014).

Certainly, boards of directors in the US and the UK in recent years have felt a more immediate responsibility to recognise a wider range of relevant constituencies as stakeholder perspectives arguably have once again become a more prominent part of corporate life (David et al. 2007; Whittaker and Deakin 2009; Clarke 2010b; Klettner et al. 2014; Clarke 2015, 2016). In US firms, recognition of the growing importance of intellectual capital, and the adoption of high-performance work practices, have all reemphasised the importance of human capital in a context where previously labour was marginalised in the interests of a single-minded shareholder ethos (Jacoby 2001: 26). It is ironic that as European and Japanese listed corporations are being forced to recognise the importance of shareholder value; Anglo-American corporations are being sharply reminded of their social responsibilities.

The widespread adoption among leading Anglo-American corporations of publishing social and environmental reports alongside their financial reports, and actively demonstrating their corporate social responsibility in other more practical ways, suggests this may be more than simply a rhetorical change (Schembera 2012; Searcy 2012). The formal adoption of *enlightened* shareholder value in the UK Companies Act indicates at least a rhetorical move forwards from the more naked pursuit of shareholder value (Keay 2013). Furthermore, unlikely evidence that the US system could in some important ways be converging towards the European model is unearthed by Thomsen (2003).

The pattern of insider ownership and extensive block holding in the US does not demarcate the American system as sharply from the European as is often suggested. And the trend may be in this direction as apparently the stock market in Anglo-American systems responds positively to higher ownership by financial institutions, and one reason for this may be the perception of better monitoring (Thomsen 2001: 310). The increasing importance of institutional investors in the US, and in every other market, means that ownership relations are once again becoming more concentrated (even if the ultimate beneficiaries are highly diffuse). This institutional ownership has begun to create forms of relational investing, which could over time lead to more exercise of voice and less of exit by US shareholders (Jacoby 2001: 26).

Much attention has been focussed upon the pressures driving large listed German corporations to focus more directly on the creation of shareholder value, and upon the insistent pressures for Japanese corporations to demonstrate more transparency and disclosure (Clarke and Chanlat 2009; Amable et al. 2012; Jackson and Sorge 2012; Seki and Clarke 2014). Less attention has been paid to the developing pressures upon Anglo-American corporations to exercise greater accountability towards institutional investors and more responsibility in relation to their stakeholder communities (Williams and Zumbansen 2011; Deeg 2012).

With multiple institutions exerting interdependent effects on firm-level outcomes (Aguilera and Jackson 2003: 448), and with different values informing the objectives for the enterprise in different cultures (Hofstede 2004), the scenario for convergence and diversity of corporate governance models is more complex and unpredictable than many commentators have suggested. A pioneer of corporate governance possessed a more compelling grasp of the possibilities that convergence and divergence may occur *simultaneously*: that is an insistent increase in diversity within an overall trend towards convergence:

Looking ahead towards the next decade it is possible to foresee a duality in the developing scenarios. On the one hand, we might expect further diversity – new patterns of ownership, new forms of group structure, new types of strategic alliance, leading to yet more alternative approaches to corporate governance. More flexible and adaptive organisational arrangements, entities created for specific projects, business ventures and task forces are likely to compound the diversity. Sharper differentiation of the various corporate governance types and the different bases for governance power will be necessary to increase the effectiveness of governance and enable the regulatory processes to respond to reality ... But on the other hand, we might expect a convergence of governance processes as large corporations operating globally, their shares traded through global financial markets, are faced with increasing regulatory convergence in company law, disclosure requirements and international accounting standards, insider trading and securities trading rules, and the exchange of information between the major regulatory bodies around the world.

(Tricker 1994: 520)

In this analysis, the strength of diversity rather than uniformity becomes apparent, even to the extent there is some convergence of regulation, and it is increasingly likely this will need to be negotiated among regions and countries rather than disseminated from the Anglo-American heartland. "There is then value in maintaining international diversity in corporate governance systems, so that we do not foreclose future alternatives and evolutionary possibilities. The argument resembles the argument for biodiversity in species" (McDonnell 2002: 18). The importance of diversity for the exercise of choice and creativity is paramount and reveals the dangers involved in national and international policy-making vigorously advocating a one-size-fits-all prescription for corporate governance (McDonnell 2002: 19). Indeed, this essential dynamism of corporate governance was fully recognised in the OECD Business Advisory Group's report at the time of the formulation of the original OECD principles:

Entrepreneurs, investors and corporations need the flexibility to craft governance arrangements that are responsive to unique business contexts so that corporations can respond to incessant changes in technologies, competition, optimal firm organization and vertical networking patterns. A market for governance arrangements should be permitted so that these arrangements that can attract investors and other resource contributors – and support competitive corporations – flourish. To obtain governance diversity, economic regulations, stock exchange rules and corporate law should support a range of ownership and governance forms. Over time, availability of "off the shelf" solutions will offer benefits of market familiarity and learning, judicial enforceability and predictability.

(OECD 1998: 34)

Future Trends

Contemplating the future of corporate governance systems is a hazardous business. Each of the systems is facing pressures to change. The long-term stakeholder orientation of the German and Japanese governance systems is under insistent pressure to deliver shareholder value, particularly from overseas investment institutions. However, the market-oriented short-termism of the Anglo-American approach is itself being challenged by international, national, and community agencies to recognise wider social and environmental responsibilities. The German and Japanese systems are faced with demands for increased transparency and disclosure from both regulators and investors, while Anglo-American corporations are faced with repeated calls for greater accountability from institutional investors and other stakeholder communities.

Bratton and McCahery (1999: 30) recognised four possible outcomes from the present pressures to converge, and the resilient institutional resistance encountered:

i   a *unitary system* as there is strong convergence towards a global system which assembles the best elements of both major governance systems and combines them together (the least likely alternative);
ii   a *universal market-based system* as anticipated by the Chicago School of financial economists, representing the triumph of the rules-based outsider system;
iii an *improved variety of governance systems* in which there is weak convergence, but some learning from each other between the different national systems;
iv   a set of *viable distinctive governance systems*, based on distinctive institutional complementarity each having a unique identity and capability.

Contrary to all of the predictions of an early and complete convergence of corporate governance systems, the final two alternatives are the closest to the present state of play, and are likely to be for some time to come, as this differentiated system has proven robustness and usefulness, reflecting different industrial strengths and strategic directions. The immense capacity of the international finance institutions to continue to drive economic and social change in their own interests should be recognised, and the increasing financialisation of corporations globally disciplined to narrower and narrower financial objectives is a plausible scenario.

The continuing threat to the variety and distinctiveness of regional forms of corporate governance and strategy should be recognised. However, Anglo-American financial institutions, even if untamed by post-crisis regulation, are under some constraint by the widespread popular demand that they demonstrate greater social responsibility (Clarke 2010b, 2016). Secondly, as presently in China, regional financial systems with different orientations and objectives to the Western banks may exert increasing influence (and indeed Chinese corporations have benefited from this radically different regime in their rapid advance).

Complexity of Corporate Governance Forms

It is likely the campaign to raise standards of corporate governance will continue for some time in all jurisdictions of the world. There will be a strenuous effort to secure commitment to the essential basis of trust identified by the OECD as fairness, transparency, accountability, and responsibility. However, this will occur in countries with different cultures, legal systems, economic priorities, and social commitments. This campaign to raise standards of accountability in corporate governance should be distinguished from the intense and numbing assault by international financial interests to impose on the corporations of the world a narrow and self-interested shareholder value ideology which will serve to constrain corporations' purpose and development.

To assume that all countries will adapt to the same corporate governance structures is unrealistic, unfounded, and unimaginative. It is likely that fundamental features of the European and Asian approaches to corporate governance will be maintained, even where the apparatus of market-based corporate governance are formally adopted. Often these differences will be perceived as part of the cultural integrity and economic dynamism of the economy in question. To the extent countries adopt universal principles, they will do so within a culturally diverse set of corporate values, structures, objectives and practices. This is part of the evolving and dynamic complexity of corporate life, in which both convergence and divergence can occur simultaneously. As pressures to conform to international standards and expectations increase, the resilience of historical and cultural differences will continue. The business case for diversity is, if anything, even more compelling. There will be a continual need to innovate around new technologies, processes, and markets. This will stimulate new organisational and corporate forms, the shape and objectives of which will be hard to predetermine.

References

Aguilera, R. and Jackson, G. (2003) The Cross-National Diversity of Corporate Governance: Dimensions and Determinants, *Academy of Management Review*, 28(3): 447–465.

Aguilera, R., Desender, K.A. and de Castro, L.R.K. (2012) A Bundle Perspective to Comparative Corporate Governance, in T. Clarke and D. Branson (eds.), *Sage Handbook of Corporate Governance*, London: Sage. 370–405.

Amable, B., Guillaud, E. and Palombarini, S. (2012) Changing French Capitalism: Political and Systemic Crises in France, *Journal of European Public Policy*, 19(8): 1168–1187.

Avgouleas, E. (2013) Rationales and Designs to Implement an Institutional Big Bang in the Governance of Global Finance, *Seattle University Law Review*, 36: 321.

Bebchuk, L.A. and Roe, M.J. (1999) A Theory of Path Dependence in Corporate Ownership and Governance, *Stanford Law Review*, 52: 127–170.

Berglöf, E. and von Thadden, E.-L. (1999) The Changing Corporate Governance Paradigm: Implications for Transition and Developing Countries (June 1999). Available at SSRN: https://ssrn.com/abstract=183708 or https://doi.org/10.2139/ssrn.183708

Branson, D. (2001) The Very Uncertain Prospects of 'Global' Convergence in Corporate Governance, *Cornell International Law Journal*, 34: 321–362.

Bratton, W.W. and McCahery, J.A. (1999) Comparative Corporate Governance and the Theory of the Firm: The Case against Global Cross Reference, *Columbia Journal of Transnational Law*, 38: 213–297.

Burghof, H.P. and Hunger, A. (2003) Access to Stock Markets for Small and Medium Sized Growth Firms: The Temporary Success and Ultimate Failure of Germany's Neuer Markt, http://www.ipo-underpricing.com/Downloads/Hunger/Hunger_Access.pdf

CCMR (2006) *Interim Report of the Committee on Capital Markets Regulation*, US Committee on Capital Markets Regulation.

Cernat, L. (2004) The Emerging European Corporate Governance Model: Anglo-Saxon, Continental or Still the Century of Diversity? *Journal of European Public Policy*, 11(1): 147–166.

Claessens, S. and Fan, J.P.H. (2002) Corporate Governance in Asia, *International Review of Finance*, 3(2): 71–103.

Clarke, T. and Bostock, R. (1994) International Corporate Governance: Convergence and Diversity, in, T. Clarke and E. Monkhouse, *Rethinking the Company,* London: Financial Times Pitman, 245–278.

Clarke, T. (2010a) Recurring Crises in Anglo-American Corporate Governance, *Contributions to Political Economy*, Oxford University Press, 29(1): 9–32.

Clarke, T. (2010b) The Materiality of Sustainability: Corporate Social and Environmental Responsibility as Instruments of Strategic Change? in J. Moon, M. Orlitzky and G. Whelan (eds.), *Governance and Business Ethics*, Cheltenham: Edward Elgar. 524–542.

Clarke, T. (2013) Deconstructing the Mythology of Shareholder Value, *Accounting, Economics, and Law*, 3(1): 15–42.

Clarke, T. (2014) The Impact of Financialisation on International Corporate Governance, *Law and Financial Markets Review*, 8(1): March 2014, 39–51.

Clarke, T. (2016) The Widening Scope of Directors Duties: The Increasing Impact of Corporate Social and Environmental Responsibility, *Seattle University Law Review*, 39(2): 557–602.

Clarke, T. and Bostock, R. (1994) International Corporate Governance: Convergence and Diversity, in T. Clarke and E. Monkhouse (eds.), *Rethinking the Company*, London: Financial Times Pitman, 345–374.

Clarke, T. and Branson, D. (eds.) (2012) *The Sage Handbook of Corporate Governance*, London and Los Angeles: Sage.

Clarke, T. (2013) Deconstructing the Mythology of Shareholder Value, *Accounting, Economics, and Law*, 3, 1, pp 15–42

Clarke, T. (2014a) The Impact of Financialisation on International Corporate Governance, *Law and Financial Markets Review*, Vol 8, Number 1, March 2014, pp 39–51

Clarke, T. (2016) 'The Widening Scope of Directors Duties: The Increasing I.mpact of Corporate Social and Environmental Responsibility, *Seattle University Law Review*, 39(2): 557–602.

Clarke, T. and dela Rama, M. (2006) *Corporate Governance and Globalisation*, Volume 1 Ownership and Control, London: Sage.

Clarke, T. and Klettner, A. (2011) Corporate Governance and the Global Financial Crisis: The Regulatory Responses, in C. Ingley and A. Tourani-Rad (eds.), *Handbook of Current Issues in Corporate Governance*, Singapore: World Scientific Publishing. 71–102.

Coffee, J. (2001) The Rise of Dispersed Ownership: The Role of the Law in the Separation of Ownership and Control, *Yale Law Journal*, 111(1).

Coffee, J. (2002) Convergence and Its Critics: What are the Preconditions to the Separation of Ownership and Control?, in J.A. McCahery, P. Moerland, T. Raaijmakers and L. Renneboog (eds.), *Corporate Governance Regimes: Convergence and Diversity*, Oxford: Oxford University Press.

Coombes, P. and Watson, M. (2000) Three Surveys on Corporate Governance, *McKinsey Quarterly*, McKinsey Corporation, 4: 74–77.

David, P., Bloom, M. and Hillman, A.J. (2007) Investor Activism, Managerial Responsiveness and Corporate Social Performance, *Strategic Management Journal*, 28: 91–100.

Davis, G.F. (2009) *Managed by the Markets: How Finance Re-shaped America*, Oxford: Oxford University Press.

Deeg, R. (2012) The limits of Liberalization? American Capitalism at the Crossroads, *Journal of European Public Policy*, 19(8): 1249–1268.

Deeg, R. and Jackson, R. (2007) Towards a More Dynamic Theory of Capitalist Variety, *Socio-Economic Review*, 5(1): 149–179.

Dore, R. (2000) *Stock Market Capitalism: Welfare Capitalism*, Oxford: Oxford University Press.

Dore, R. (2002) Will Global Capitalism Be Anglo-Saxon Capitalism?, *Asian Business & Management*, 1(1): 9–18.6

Dore, R. (2008) Financialization of the Global Economy 17, *Industrial and Corporate Change*, 17(6): 1097–1112.

Epstein, G. (2005) (ed.), *Financialization and the World Economy*, Cheltenham: Edward Elgar.

European Commission (2005) *The EU Economy 2005 Review: Rising International Integration – Opportunities and Challenges*, Commission of the European Communities, Director General Economic and Financial Affairs, Brussels, European Commision.

Fligstein, N. and Freeland, R. (1995) Theoretical and Comparative Perspectives on Corporate Organization, *Annual Review of Sociology*, 21: 21–43.

Fukuyama, F. (1996) *Trus: The Social Values and the Creation of Property*, New York: Free Press.

Gilson, R. (2000) Globalizing Corporate Governance: Convergence of Form or Function, *Columbia Law School the Center for Law and Economic Studies* (Working Paper February 2000).

Gordon, J.N. and Roe, M.J. (2004) *Convergence and Persistence in Corporate Governance*, Cambridge: Cambridge University Press.

Goyer, M. and Jung, D.K. (2011) Diversity of Institutional Investors and Foreign Blockholdings in France, *Corporate Governance: An International Review*, 19: 562–584.

Gunter, B.G. and van der Hoeven, R. (2004) The Social Dimension of Globalization: A Review of the Literature, *Working Paper Number 24*, World Commission on the Social Dimensions of Globalization, Geneva: International Labour Office.

Hamilton, D.S. and Quinlan, J.P. (2005) *Deep Integration: How Transatlantic Markets are Leading Globalisation*, Brussels: Centre for European Policy Studies.

Hancké, B. (eds.) (2009) *Debating Varieties of Capitalism*, Oxford: Oxford University Press.

Hancké, B., Rhodes, M. and Thatcher, M. (2007) *Beyond Varieties of Capitalism Conflict, Contradictions, and Complementarities in the European Economy*, Oxford: Oxford University Press.

Hansmann, H. and Kraakman, R. (2001) The End of History for Corporate Law, *Georgetown Law Journal*, 89: 439.

Hofstede, G. (2004) Business Goals and Corporate Governance, *Asian Pacific Business Review*, 10(3–4): 292–301.

Jackson, G. and Deeg, R. (2012) The Long-Term Trajectories of Institutional Change in European Capitalism, *Journal of European Public Policy*, 19(8): 1109–1125.

Jackson, G. and Sorge, A. (2012) The Trajectory of Institutional Change in Germany, 1979–2009, *Journal of European Public Policy*, 19(8): 1146–1167.

Jacoby, S. (2001) Corporate Governance in Comparative Perspective: Prospects for Convergence, *Comparative Labour Law and Policy Journal*, 22(1): 5–28.

Jacoby, S. (2007) *The Embedded Corporation: Corporate Governance and Employment Relations in Japan and the United States*, Princeton, NJ: Princeton University Press.

Jesovar, F. and Kirkpatrick, G. (2005) The Revised OECD Principles of Corporate Governance and their Relevance to Non-OECD Countries, *Corporate Governance – An International Review*, 13(2): 127–136.

Keay, A. (2013) *The Enlightened Shareholder Value Principle and Corporate Governance*, London: Routledge.

Klettner, K., Clarke, T. and Boersma, M. (2014) The Governance of Corporate Sustainability: Empirical Insights into the Development, Leadership and Implementation of Responsible Business Strategy, *Journal of Business Ethics*, 122(1): 145–165.

Kobrin, S.J. (2002) Economic Governance in an Electronically Networked Global Economy, in R.H. Bruce and T.J. Biersteker (eds.), *The Emergence of Private Authority in Global Governance*, New York: Cambridge University Press, 43–76.

Krippner, G. (2005) The Financialization of the American Economy, *Socio-Economic Review*, 3: 173–208.

Krippner, G. (2012) *Capitalizing on Crisis: The Political Origins of the Rise of Finance*, Cambridge, MA: Harvard University Press.

La Porta, R., Lopez-de-Silanes, F. et al. (1998) Law and Finance, *Journal of Political Economy*, 106(6): 1113–1155.

La Porta, R., Lopez-de-Silanes, F. and Shleifer, Al. (1999) Corporate Ownership around the World, *Journal of Finance*, 54(2): 471–517.

La Porta, R., Lopez-de-Silanes, F., Shleifer, A. and Vishny, R. (2000) Investor Protection and Corporate Governance, *Journal of Financial Economics*, 58(1): 3–27.

La Porta, R., Lopez-De-Silanes, F., Shleifer, A. and Vishny, R. (2002) Investor Protection and Corporate Valuation, *Journal of Finance*, 57(3): 1147–1170.

Lane, C. (2003). Changes in Corporate Governance of German Corporations: Convergence to the Anglo-American Model? *Competition and Change*, 7(2): 79–100.

Lazonick, W. (1992) Controlling the Market for Corporate Control: The Historical Significance of Managerial Capitalism, Industrial and Corporate Change, 1(3): 445–488.

Lazonick, W. (2012) In the Name of Shareholder Value: How Executive Pay and Stock Buy-Backs Are Damaging the US Economy, in T. Clarke and D. Branson (eds.), *The Sage Handbook of Corporate Governance* (pp. 476–495), London: Sage.

Lazonick, W. (2014) Profits without Prosperity, *Harvard Business Review*, September. 92(9), 46–55.

Licht, A. (2003) The Maximands of Corporate Governance: A Theory of Values and Cognitive Style, *European Corporate Governance Institute*, Law Working Paper No 16, ECGI.

Licht, A.N. (2001). The Mother of all Path Dependencies: Towards a Cross-Cultural Theory of Corporate Governance Systems, *Delaware Journal of Corporate Law*, 26: 147–209.

Lomborg, B. (2004) *Global Crises, Global Solutions*, Cambridge: Cambridge University Press.

McCahery, J.A., Moerland, P., Raaijmakers, T. and Renneboog, L. (2002). *Corporate Governance Regimes: Convergence and Diversity*. Oxford: Oxford University Press.

McDonnell, B.H. (2002). Convergence in Corporate Governance – Possible, But Not Desirable, *Villanova Law Review*, 47(2): 341–386.

Moerland, P.W. (1995). Corporate Ownership and Control Structures: An International Comparison, *Review of Industrial Organization*, 10(4): 443–464.

OECD (1998a) *Corporate Governance: Improving Competitiveness and Access to Capital in Global Markets, A Report to the OECD by the Business Sector Advisory Group on Corporate Governance*, Paris: OECD.

Pinto, A.R. (2005) Globalization and the Study of Comparative Corporate Governance, *Wisconsin International Law Journal*, 23(3): 477–504.

Rajan, R. and Zingales, L. (2003) The Great Reversals: The Politics of Financial Development in the Twentieth Century, *Journal of Financial Economics*, 69(1): 5–50

Rajan, R.R. (2010) *Hidden Fractures Still Threaten the World Economy*, Princeton, NJ: Princeton University Press.

Roe, M. (2000) Political Preconditions to Separating Ownership and Control, *Stanford Law Review*, 53: 539.

Roe, M. (2003) *Political Determinants of Corporate Governance*, Oxford: Oxford University Press.

Roe, M.J. (1994) *Strong Managers, Weak Owners: The Political Roots of American Corporate Finance*, Princeton, NJ: Princeton University Press.

Schembera, S. (2012) *Implementing Corporate Social Responsibility: Empirical Insights on the Impact and Accountability of the UN Global Compact*, University of Zurich, Business Working Paper Series, Working Paper No. 316.

Searcy, C. (2012) Corporate Sustainability Performance Measurement Systems: A Review and Research Agenda, *Journal of Business Ethics*, 107: 239–253.

Seki, T. and Clarke, T. (2014) The Evolution of Corporate Governance in Japan: The Continuing Relevance of Berle and Means, *Seattle University Law Review*, 37: 717–747.

Thomsen, S. (2001) Business Ethics as Corporate Governance, *European Journal of Law and Economics*, 11(2): 153–164.

Thomsen, S. (2003) The Convergence of Corporate Governance Systems and European and Anglo-American Standards, *European Business Organisation Law Review*, Cambridge University Press, 4: 31–50.

Tricker, R.I. (1994) *International Corporate Governance*, Singapore: Prentice Hall.

van der Zwan, N. (2013) Making Sense of Financialization, *Socio-Economic Review*, 12: 99.

von Kalckreuth, U. and Silbermann, L. (2010) Bubbles and Incentives: A Post-Mortem of the Neuer Markt in Germany, Deutsche Bundesbank, https://www.bundesbank.de/Redaktion/EN/Downloads/Publications/Disc ussion_Paper_1/2010/2010_07_23_dkp_15.pdf?__blob=publicationFile

Whittaker, D.H. and Deakin, S. (2009) *Corporate Governance and Managerial Reform in Japan*, Oxford: Oxford University Press.

Williams, C.A. and Zumbansen, P. (2011) *The Embedded Firm: Corporate Governance, Labor, and Finance Capitalism*, Cambridge: Cambridge University.

Young, R. (1997) *Restructuring Europe: An Investor's View*, New York: Goldman Sachs International.

4 Shareholder Primacy
The End of a Hegemony?

Value Creation

Important differences continue internationally in the understanding of what corporate governance concerns. The dilemmas concerning the proper role of the board of directors in strategic directions are related to the differing views regarding the purposes of value creation. As Huse and Gabrielsson (2012: 234) suggest there are markedly different views regarding the true purpose and direction of value creation by companies. Aency theorists assume value creation is primarily for shareholders and managerialists suggest it is monopolised by the interests of management. Stakeholder perspectives adopt a broader view of the purposes of value creation for all those who have made a contribution to the success of the company. Team production theories see value creation in terms of the broad interests of the firm and recognise the importance of value creation through the whole of the value chain.

To Whom Is the Board of Directors Responsible?

If the board is to play a central role in the strategic direction of the company, the underlying question is "for what purpose?" It is not possible to answer this question fully without addressing the more fundamental question of "to whom is the board responsible?" Adrian Cadbury states:

> The simple answer to this question is that boards owe their duty to their shareholders. The precise and legal answer is that directors, and therefore the boards of whom they are made up, owe their duty to the company. How real is the difference between these two concepts and does the difference matter? While serving the shareholder interest is a useful working definition of a board's duty,

DOI: 10.4324/9780429294648-4

there are situations when it may cease to hold good … First, it is clear that a company as a body corporate has a legal personality distinct from its members. A company is not, therefore, the same as its shareholders. The company is neither the agent of the share-holders nor their trustee … In effect, the shareholders of a company elect its directors and entrust them with the control of the company' affairs. From there on, the directors owe their duty to the company and in following that course they may take decisions which some or all of the shareholders consider not to be in their best interests. The recourse which the shareholders have in that situation is to exercise their powers in the general meeting to vote in a new board of directors whom they consider will look after their interests more faithfully.

(2002: 41–42)

Recognition of the distinct personality of the company is a pre-condition to the legal structure for the limited liability of the members.

The logic of separate personality and limited liability doctrines favours the externalisation of the social costs of corporate be-haviour, shifting the risk of the enterprise operations away from shareholders and onto stakeholders or wider society, whether those with firm-specific investments such as employees, suppliers and local communities or the wider community.

(Redmond 2005: 156)

The corporation has a legal personality of a different character to a natural person, since though invested with the legal capacity and powers of an individual, its incorporate nature ensures that it has perpetual succession, unaffected by change in its membership. Fur-ther differences relating to the artificial character of the corporate personality exist, as in the comment attributed to the English Lord Chancellor Thurlow in the eighteenth century: "Did you ever expect a corporation to have a conscience, when it has no soul to be damned, and no body to be kicked?" (Redmond 2005: 157).

But the corporate personality and limited liability of the public company place definite limits on the rights and powers of sharehold-ers, as Cadbury comments:

The distinction between a company and its shareholders was clearly drawn by Lord Evershed in 1947 in a case concerning compen-sation for the shareholders of Short Brothers on the compulsory acquisition of their shares in 1943: "Shareholders are not in the eye of the law, part owners of the undertaking. The undertaking is something different from the totality of the shareholdings" ... What shareholders own are *shares*. These shares acknowledge the investment which their holders have made in a company carrying on a business and confer certain rights and responsibilities on their owners. The owners are entitled to whatever dividends are declared and they have some security against the assets of the company should it be wound up. Owning shares in a company is not strictly the same as owning the business carried on by the company.

(2002: 42)

Somehow though, a conventional wisdom has been broadcast in the US and the UK that shareholders enjoy property rights over companies, and that therefore the purpose of companies is to exclusively serve shareholder interests. The fact this claim is *not* supported in law in either the US or the UK has not prevented its energetic propagation to many other jurisdictions, as Blair and Stout argue:

Commentators who use the rhetoric of property rights to justify shareholder primacy bring a strong moral overtone to their arguments, implying that any use of corporate assets that does not directly enhance shareholder wealth is a form of theft. Yet from a logical perspective, the naked claim that shareholders own the corporation is just that – a naked claim. As a legal matter, shareholders neither control how the firm's assets are used, nor are they entitled to receive dividends or make any other direct claim on the firm's earnings ... Contemporary corporate law treats corporations as separate and autonomous legal persons whose boards of directors have authority to make decisions and take action without shareholder approval ... Shareholders do not own corporate assets nor have the right to control them. *Bryan v. Aikin* 10 Del. Ch. 466, 86 A. 674 (1913) ('The stockholder does not, and cannot, own the property of the corporation, or even the earnings, until they are declared in the form of dividends.')
  Moreover, the legal rights shareholders do enjoy (e.g., the right to elect directors, to veto certain corporate transactions by majority voting, to offer proposals that the directors are often free to ignore, to receive dividends – if and when – the directors declare them) look very different from the rights enjoyed by those who "own" physical assets such as land or jewelry. As a result the assertion that shareholders are "owners" of corporations functions

primarily as a rhetorical device designed to trump all other arguments. It is not, by itself, a serious legal or economic argument.

(Blair and Stout 2001: 9; Blair 2012; Stout 2012)

Shareholder Primacy

Yet the concept of shareholder primacy, and the concomitant insistence that the only real purpose of the corporation is to deliver shareholder value, has become an almost universal principle of corporate governance in the Anglo-American world and has an increasingly insistent voice in Europe and Asia-Pacific as international institutional investors exert influence on corporations, and this often goes unchallenged (Stout 2012; Clarke 2013). This self-interested, tenacious, and simplistic belief is corrosive of any effort to realise the deeper values companies are built upon, the wider purposes they serve, and the broader set of relationships they depend upon for their success:

> For nearly as long as the public corporation has existed, the job description and legal obligations of corporate directors has been the subject of debate among scholars, practitioners, and policymakers. But to anyone who entered the debate in the last decade and read only the dominant academic commentary or informal discussions in the business press, the issue might appear to have been conclusively settled in favor of the following two propositions. First, the board's only job is to faithfully serve the interests of the firm's shareholders. Second, the best way to do this is to maximize the value of the company's shares ... The idea that shareholders alone are the *raison d'être* of the corporation has come to dominate contemporary discussion of corporate governance, both outside and (in many cases) inside the boardroom. Yet the "shareholder primacy" claim seems at odds with a variety of important characteristics of US corporate law. Despite the emphasis legal theorists have given shareholder primacy in recent years, corporate law itself does not obligate directors to do what the shareholders tell them to do. Nor does it compel the board to maximize share value. To the contrary, directors of public corporations enjoy a remarkable degree of freedom from shareholder command and control. Similarly, the law grants them wide discretion to consider the interests of other corporate participants in their decision-making – even when this adversely affects the value of the stockholders' shares.

(Blair and Stout 2001: 5)

The obsessive emphasis on shareholder value is an ideology that is constricting and misleading in business enterprise, and is intended to crowd out other relevant and viable strategies for business success:

> Shareholder primacy is both positively and normatively incorrect – at least in the extreme rhetorical form in which it is most commonly expressed. Corporate law does not (nor should it) require directors to maximize the value of the company's common stock. To the contrary, it grants (and should grant) the directors of public companies enormous freedom to decide where and how the firm ought to allocate its scarce resources. This arrangement does not *preclude* corporate directors from using their autonomy to pursue a higher stock price. However, it also does not prevent them from using the firm's resources instead to benefit managers, employees, or even the local community.
>
> (Blair and Stout 2001: 6)

The Corporation as a Complex Social Institution

In the *UK Modern Company Law Review* (UK DTI 2000), John Parkinson argued the case for a more pluralist conception of the purposes of the corporation. This view refutes Anglo-American conception of the company as simply property, or the product of contracting between various participants in the business, which characterise the company as "private" and consider it should be run exclusively in the interests of shareholders. This resonates more with the European tradition that economically significant companies are to a degree public bodies which have extensive constituencies that include employees and local communities (Parkinson 2003: 481):

> The idea that the company is a complex social institution which cannot adequately be characterized through the language of ownership or contract. Instead, this perspective introduces concepts such as citizenship, participation and legitimacy, which depart from the concerns of both private property rights and conventional economic analysis. The suggestion is that these values, which have more usually been applied to non-commercial, social and political organizations, are appropriate too in evaluating the governance of firms and in making recommendations for their reform.
>
> (Parkinson 2003: 491)

The *UK Modern Company Law Review* (UK DTI 2000) asked: "What should be the legal rule with respect to directors' duties?" Should company law

- require directors and senior managers to act by reference to the interests of all stakeholders in the corporate enterprise, according to primacy to no particular interests including those of shareholders (mandatory pluralism)?
- permit (but not require) directors and senior managers to act by reference to the interests of all stakeholders, according to primacy to no particular interests including those of shareholders (discretionary pluralism)?

The most radical of these models is the mandatory pluralist model, creating a multi-fiduciary duty requiring directors and managers to run the company in the interest of all those with a stake in its success; balancing the claims of shareholders, employees, suppliers, the community, and other stakeholders. The claims of each stakeholder are recognised as valuable in their own right and no priority is accorded to shareholders in this adjustment; their interest may be sacrificed to that of other stakeholders. The discretionary pluralist model would permit, but not require, directors to sacrifice shareholder interests to those of other stakeholders. Either of these models would formalise earlier managerialist practice that has been displaced by the current shareholder value culture.

The review process and the subsequent *Company Law Reform Bill* attempted to tread a fine legal line between a sense of "enlightened shareholder value," which was becoming best practice in many leading U.K. and international companies, and more radical claims for company law to adopt a more "pluralist" sense of the ultimate objectives of the enterprise and the interests to be served. The reform attempted to manage this balancing act by suggesting that the pluralist objectives of maximising company performance to the benefit of all stakeholders can best be served by professional directors pursuing commercial opportunities within a framework of standards and accountability:

> The overall objective should be pluralist in the sense that companies should be run in a way which maximises overall competitiveness and wealth and welfare for all. But the means which company law deploys for achieving this objective must be to take account of the realities and dynamics which operate in practice in the running of commercial enterprise. It should not be done

at the expense of turning company directors from business decisions makers into moral, political or economic arbiters, but by
harnessing focused, comprehensive competitive decision making
within robust, objective professional standards and flexible, but
pertinent, accountability.

(UK DTI 2000)

After much debate, it was the discretionary pluralism model that
emerged clearly in the UK. Company Law Review Steering Group following its comprehensive review of company law, which recommended
a recasting of directors' duties to give effect to its notion of *enlightened
shareholder value* ultimately contained in the Companies Bill 2006,
which received Royal Assent on November 8, 2006.

Section 172(1) of the *UK Companies Act 2006* establishes a duty to
pursue broadly the success of the company:

172   Duty to promote the success of the company

1   A director of a company must act in the way he considers, in good
faith, would be most likely to promote the success of the company
for the benefit of its members as a whole, and in doing so have
regard (amongst other matters) to

a   the likely consequences of any decision in the long term;
b   the interests of the company's employees;
c   the need to foster the company's business relationships with
suppliers, customers, and others'
d   the impact of the company's operations on the community
and the environment;
e   the desirability of the company maintaining a reputation for
high standards of business conduct; and
f   the need to act fairly as between members of the company
(*Companies Act*, 2006, c. 46, § 172 (UK (2006) *Companies Act
2006*).

Yet, not only in the UK, but also in the US, this controversial new
clause was trumpeted as a remarkable innovation in company law, the
UK government claiming the provision "marks a radical departure in
articulating the connection between what is good for a company and
what is good for society at large." How the government interpreted the
new clause was elaborated in the 2005 White Paper:

The basic goal for directors should be the success of the company
for the benefit of its members as a whole; but that, to reach this

goal, directors would need to take a properly balanced view of the implications of decisions over time and foster effective relationships with employees, customers and suppliers, and in the community more widely. The Government strongly agrees that this approach, which [is] called "enlightened shareholder value," is most likely to drive long-term company performance and maximise overall competitiveness and wealth and welfare for all.

(UK DTI 2005: 3.3)

The Continuing Compulsion of Shareholder Value

The hope that a more responsible approach to corporate direction might issue from the *enlightened shareholder value* principles of the UK Companies Act were quickly dashed. This was despite strong resonances between the principles espoused and the earlier traditions of many UK and US corporations. Historically, American corporations have demonstrated a broad conception of the orientation towards a wide constituency of stakeholders necessary in order to build the enterprise. Over time and with the increasing market power of large corporations, managements' sense of accountability might have become overwhelmed by complacency and self-interest. However, to attempt to replace self-interested managers, with managers keenly focused entirely upon delivering value to shareholders, is to replace one form of self-interest with another.

Any broadening of the social obligations of the company was dangerous according to the shareholder value school of thought, "Few trends could so thoroughly undermine the foundations of our free society as the acceptance by corporate officials of a social responsibility other than to make as much money for their stockholders as possible" (Friedman 1962: 113; Clarke 2020). The difficulty is whether in trying to represent the interests of all stakeholders, company directors simply slip the leash of the one truly effective restraint that regulates their behaviour – their relationship with shareholders. These views were expressed with vigour by liberal economists and enjoyed the support of leading business leaders and senior politicians. More practically, such views reflected how US and UK companies were driven in the period of the 1980s and 1990s, and often continue to be driven in this way in the present day, with an emphasis upon sustaining share price and dividend payments at all costs, and freely using merger and takeover activity to discipline managers who failed in their responsibility to enhance shareholder value. It was the economic instability and insecurity created by this approach that was criticised in the report by Porter (1992) on how the US capital markets were eviscerating the US manufacturing industry.

Monks and Minow attempted a restating of the essential principles of the shareholder theory of the firm, which is more tolerant of the interests of other constituents, but insists they are best served by acknowledging the supremacy of the ultimate owner (2001: 40). But it could be questioned whether a singular focus upon shareholder interests really is the key to sustainable corporate performance and effective accountability. In an era of increasing participation of consumers, environmental, employees, and other economic groups, to assume that shareholders alone are capable of effective monitoring is untenable. An irony is that shareholders, particularly the scattered army of individual shareholders, have not been particularly well looked after or informed in the recent past, even by companies espousing shareholder value views, and particularly in the US which is the home of shareholder value philosophy. Who then does the shareholder value ideology benefit?

Deakin (2005) examines how the market for corporate control in the 1980s used the takeover mechanism as the catalyst to ensure managers of large corporations acted in the interests of shareholders. Many of the measures developed during this era have now been internalised in companies, for example, the near-universal adoption by listed companies of the accounting metrics of earnings per share, economic value added, and returns on capital employed which in various ways benchmark corporate performance by reference to shareholder returns. However, the enthusiasm of top executives for these measures corresponds closely with them receiving an increasing amount of their reward in stock options:

> Share option schemes, from a small beginning in the mid-1980s, are now a near universal feature of executive pay in large US and UK corporations. Share options represented a revolution in the way senior managers were paid and incentivised. In the immediate post-war period, professional managers often did not own shares (let alone have options to purchase shares) in the companies they ran; indeed, separation from the concerns of shareholders was often viewed in a positive light. With the advent of share options, as managers saw their own wealth increasingly tied up with that of the company's share price, managerial attitudes also began to change. Fewer of the leaders of large corporations were engineering or technical experts in their field; instead accounting, legal and financial skills were now the most highly valued. The goal of the senior managerial class with the goal of share price maximisation has thereby become even more complete.
>
> (Deakin 2005: 14)

Financially driven managers fitted well into an increasingly powerful financially driven market environment of the 1990s with equity values, targets of current and future earnings, and an intensified interest in share price against the background of the longest bull market and economic upswing in history. This *financialisation* of business activity in the Anglo-American regime denoted a profound change in orientation involving a concentration on financial results, with a shift of focus from production markets to capital markets, with the danger of the concentrated forces of the capital market far more mobile and threatening, than the old forces of the product market of dispersed consumers. This shift in focus had great implications for the competitiveness of much of the US and UK manufacturing industries in the 1980s and was to provide an unstable platform for future business development (Froud et al. 2000). An excessive focus on immediate market returns often serves to simply increase the extent and cynicism of market manipulation (Redmond 2005: 854).

At times in the 1970s and 1980s, it appeared that the market-based shareholder value orientation was damaging the US and UK economies as the relentless pursuit of short-term returns was associated with downsizing, loss of market share, and sometimes the abandoning of whole industries to overseas competitors with longer investment horizons. Towards the end of this period, Michael Porter (1992) wrote a report for the US Council on Competitiveness on *Capital Disadvantage: America's Failing Capital Investment System*, in which he contrasted the *fluid* capital investment system of the US, with the *dedicated* capital investment system of Germany and Japan.

While the US system focused purely on financial goals and measures and short-term performance, the German and Japanese systems were characterised by long-term investment in industrial strategies to boost productivity and capability. However, as the industrial fortunes of the respective countries appeared to reverse in the 1990s, these lessons were forgotten, and shareholder value ideology was mightily reinforced as the unquestioned doctrine of the western corporate world.

It was in the hollowing-out of the social responsibility of business that the US business corporation emerged as primarily a financial instrument. In this new financialised, de-materialised, and de-humanised corporate world agency theory could be purveyed as the primary theoretical explanation, and shareholder value as the ultimate objective with impunity. In turn, these new conceptions of the theory and objective of the firm became vital ingredients in the further financialisation of corporations, markets, and economies (Weinstein 2012; 2013).

The consequences for corporate America of the systemic application of shareholder value were revealed in Bill Lazonick's research on innovation: US corporations hoard trillions of dollars, and will only spend money on dividends, share buybacks, and executive options – all designed to enhance their share price. Disastrously, investment in innovation, product, and skill development collapsed in the US industry (with the notable exceptions of the large platform technology corporations of Apple, Google, Amazon, and Facebook that now dominate the NASDAQ). Business innovation is fuelled by investment. Innovation trajectories are shaped not simply by new knowledge and technical capability but also by the rates and criteria by which financial markets and institutions will allocate resources to innovative business enterprise. Long-term innovation and investment performance requires attention to more than short-term financial metrics to satisfy the most transient of shareholders (Lazonick 2009, 2012).

Shareholder Value Maximisation as an Instrument for Compounding Inequality

Ultimately shareholder value becomes primarily an instrument for compounding existing inequality: "to anyone who has worked for a corporation or observed the ways that corporations can externalise some of their costs onto employees, customers, or the communities where they operate, the idea that "maximising share value is equivalent to maximising the total social value created by the firm" seems obviously wrong. The long-run maximisation of share value is not the equivalent to maximising total social value." On the contrary, the in-the-long-run argument simply

> fails to make a case that shareholders' interest should be given precedence over other legitimate interests and goals of the corporation ... Neither in theory nor in practice, is it true that maximizing the value of equity shares is the equivalent of maximizing the overall value created by the firm.
>
> (Blair quoted by Ireland 2005 p. 143)

This suggests that shareholder primacy is more accurately seen as a device for achieving a particular distribution of the product of productive activity than as a mechanism for achieving economic efficiency. Its vigorous re-assertion, like the adoption of neo-liberal policies more generally, involves

> a shift in the internal social relationships within states in favour of creditor and rentier interests, with the subordination of productive

sectors to financial sectors and with a drive to shift wealth and power and security away from the bulk of the working population.
(Ireland 2005: 31)

In this way, the core purpose of business enterprise in the Anglo-American world has radically shifted from the creation of wealth for all stakeholders in the corporate endeavour to share, to the extraction of value from the activity of the enterprise for a select group of financial institutions, shareholders, and executives exclusively to enjoy. In this tragic inversion of the purposes of enterprise, the structural increasing inequality of wealth now disfiguring Western economies is born (Davis 2009; Reich 2016). While other important causes of increasing structural inequality have been recognised including "the financialization of economies that has taken place since 1990, inequality increased because labour flexibility intensified, labour market institutions weakened as trade unions lost power, and public social spending started to retrench and did not compensate the vulnerabilities created by the globalization process" (Tridico and Fadda 2018: 2), shareholder value has proved a powerful and unrecognised driver of intensifying inequality internationally (Clarke and Boersma 2017; Hickel 2017).

As the Board of Governors of the Federal Reserve (2014) indicate the ownership of all financial assets in the US is heavily skewed towards the top 5 per cent of the population who by 2013 possessed more than 60 per cent of these assets, while the bottom 50 per cent of the population barely have any financial assets (Figure 4.1). Wolf (2002) highlights that US financial securities and business equity are the most heavily skewed financial assets in their distribution, with just 1 per cent of the population owning 64 per cent of financial securities and the next 9 per cent of the population owning 30 per cent of these assets. Similarly, 1 per cent of the U.S. population own 61 per cent of business equity and the next 9 per cent of the population own 31 per cent of business equity.

Therefore, in essence, the elevated mantra of the maximisation of shareholder value effectively boils down to devoting corporations to the financial interests of 1 per cent of the U.S. population, and at best 10 per cent of the population. That is shareholder value behind the elaborate pretension is essentially a creed of maximising intense and increasing inequality to the benefit of a tiny percentage of the population. The crudeness of the avarice and recklessness that underlies the maximisation of shareholder value is most clearly demonstrated in the massive, continuing, and irresponsible inflation in executive pay during the last three decades.

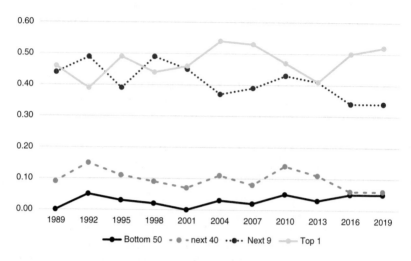

Figure 4.1 Share of All Financial Assets by Net Worth Group in US

The Explosion of Executive Pay

It is important to remember that though hundreds of millions of dollars are routinely paid individually to the leading CEOs and financial institution executives in the US, and though the country remains the second richest in GDP (after China), the political economy of the US is deeply disfigured by the mounting, severe, and very visible inequality. While CEO salaries inflated through the roof in the era from the 1990s to the present day, average earnings in America actually went down (EPI 2015). In this re-invention of inequality, the US led the world: "The share of total income going to top income groups has risen dramatically in recent decades in the United States and in many other (but not all) countries" (Atkinson et al. 2011: 6). How did this insistent inequality reappear in the industrial world, what are its causes, and what are the consequences?

Executive remuneration began to explode in the late 1980s and early 1990s when executives began to be encouraged to align their thinking more closely with shareholders by receiving equity-based pay. Jensen and Murphy (1990) asked the rhetorical question "Why pay executives like bureaucrats?". The apparent answer to this question was to load executives up with equity pay until this became the lion's share of their remuneration (Hall 2003). The purpose was to focus and enhance executive's performance on achieving returns to shareholders: equity-based compensation was intended as the silver bullet to achieve higher rates of shareholder value. However, the critical flaw in this plan is that executives were running the company and could influence the performance of the company to serve their own purposes, and effectively seize control of their own reward structures:

> Flawed compensation arrangements have not been limited to a small number of "bad apples"; they have been widespread, persistent and systemic. Furthermore, the problems have not resulted from temporary mistakes or lapses of judgement that boards can be expected to correct on their own; rather they have stemmed from structural defects in the underlying governance structure that enables executives to exert considerable influence over their boards. The absence of effective arm's-length dealing under today's system of corporate governance has been the primary source of problematic compensation arrangements. Finally, while recent reforms that seek to increase board independence will likely improve matters, they will not be sufficient to make boards adequately accountable; much more needs to be done.
>
> (Bebchuk and Fried 2005: 2)

During the boom years of the 1990s, there was a rapid and sustained escalation in CEO salaries in the United States, and any expected adjustment downwards in executive reward with the market crash of 2001, and the halving of the market capitalisation of many large corporations, did not occur. These extravagant salary packages were readily disengaged from any meaningful incentive system and became instead bullish self-justificatory status symbols. Though there were more stringent efforts to link CEO compensation to performance, US CEO rewards remained at incredibly high levels whether the companies they managed did well or not. Extremely lucrative share option schemes continued, and if the options packages became more sophisticated, there were many devices such as backdating widely employed to ensure executives extracted the best possible reward from their options. This pattern has continued to the present day: whatever reductions in their remuneration (if any) CEOs experienced during the financial crisis were quickly restored in the period after the crisis, and soon were as extravagant as they had ever been before. Stock options in the US proved the route to enriching not just brilliant software entrepreneurs but any CEO of an S&P 100 company who stayed in office long enough to massage the company accounts.

The total remuneration package paid to CEOs in the US included base salary, bonuses, benefits, long-term incentive plans, and profits from cashing out on stock options where this information was accessible. U.S. executive salaries are by far the most inflated in the world, followed by the UK. Executive salaries in Europe are generally more modest, and in Japan are much lower (though the example of US executive excess is influencing the behaviour of executives in other economies) (Clarke 2017; Clarke et al. 2019). Claims that such extravagant salaries are required to incentivise US CEOs and create greater alignment between their interests and those of the shareholders scarcely stand scrutiny: despite the sophisticated formulas often employed in complex compensation packages, all too often extravagant CEO salaries have little connection to performance measured in terms of shareholder returns, peer performance, or any measure of stakeholder values.

Of course, CEO salaries are only a part of wider structures of inequality that have become more extreme in recent years, and rewards for executives in the finance sector have become even more astronomically inflated with billions of dollars being paid to the small group of top hedge fund directors. (When the leaders of the hedge funds were hauled into the U.S. Congress House Committee investigating the financial crisis George Soros admitted that "more regulation of the financial system is needed in order to reign in the greed that ultimately creates unsustainable economic bubbles" *New York Times* 13 November 2008.)

As Thomas Piketty's *Capital in the 21st Century* (2014) graphically demonstrates western economies led by the US have been drifting back into levels of inequality not witnessed since the nineteenth century. The irony is that as the US has become one of the most unequal societies in the world, there has been a rediscovery of philanthropy, with both Bill Gates and Warren Buffet eager to give most of their vast $100+ billion fortunes away to help solve the most deep-seated problems of the world. Mark Zuckerberg has responded to this by channelling some company stock and his own money into public education. But earlier in the twentieth century, both corporations and individuals were taxed at a level that enabled governments to meet these problems of social need and equality of opportunity, without having to depend on the largesse of the super-rich.

The essential problem is not the unrestrained and absolute growth in CEO reward, however morally dubious that is in organisations where CEOs are expected to be setting an example of ethical behaviour rather than greed, it is the wider impact of the obsessive focus on CEO reward systems in Anglo-American corporations. Firstly, there is the debilitating displacement of goals as the *objectives* of the corporation under the leadership of equity incentivised CEOs switches from the single-minded focus on the development and success of the company to highly individualistic CEO strategies on how to align the performance of the corporation with the maximisation of their personal earnings. Secondly, how the arrogation of an increasing share of the wealth of the corporation by the CEO impacts upon *relationships* with other employees, shareholders, and the wider community, as CEOs become increasingly remote from the material concerns of the rest of the people and disinterested in serving them.

The displacement of CEO goals is not a recent problem but occurred in earlier periods in different forms, for example, in earlier periods of merger and takeover activity, often the most insistent driver was CEOs' ambition, since they associated acquisitions with higher rewards for themselves, regardless of the consequences for other employees. Similarly, the sustained lack of capital investment in the US and UK industries in the 1970s and 1980s was partly due to the self-interest of management:

> The problem was not only the high cost and mobility of capital. The problem was also the willingness of many top managers of industrial corporations to take advantage of the permissive financial environment to appropriate huge levels of compensation for themselves while neglecting to build organizational capabilities in the companies they were supposed to lead.
>
> (Lazonick 1992: 476)

However, the displacement of goals since the introduction of equity-based pay for CEOs has become systemic, and now agreeing the elaborate design of the CEO remuneration package is one of the principal roles of boards of directors. For example, in the celebrated downfall of WorldCom, the report prepared for the District Court of New York stated: "The Audit Committee spent as little as six hours per year in overseeing the activities of a company with more than $30 billion in revenue, while the WorldCom Compensation Committee met as often as 17 times per year" (Breeden 2003: 31).

As critical as the detachment of US executives from their corporations and shareholders' interests that occurred since the 1990s was the distance that grew between the rewards and lifestyle of executives and their employees and other stakeholders. In 1965, the ratio of CEO and worker compensation in the US in the top 350 US firms by sales was approximately 21:1, and by 1989, this had risen to a ratio of 61:1. With the meteoric rise in executive pay in the 1990s, the ratio expanded inexorably to an unprecedented 366:1 in the stock market bubble of

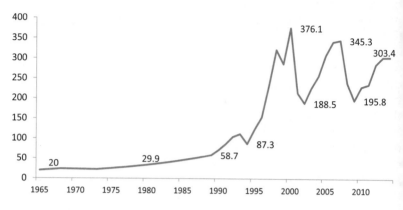

Figure 4.2 CEO to Worker Compensation Ratio in the US, 1965–2014

2000 (Figure 4.2). After the fall-out from the Enron and WorldCom in 2001/2002 and the introduction of the Sarbanes Oxley regulation, the ratio falls down to 250:1. The corporate excesses quickly recover in the security-fuelled frenzy of excess that led to the global financial crisis of 2008/09. The post-crisis regulatory intervention put a check of executive excess for a short while in both cases, but with the public stimulus led recovery CEO salaries returned quickly to an inflated ratio of 350:1 by 2020 compared to worker pay (Figure 4.2).

Though there was productivity growth during this era, almost all the benefits went to top management: as Dew-Becker and Gordon who examined the distribution of the benefits of growth in the US comment:

> Our results show the dominant share of real income gains accruing to the top 10 per cent and top 1 per cent is almost as large for labour income as total income ... It is not that all gains went to capital and none to labour; rather, our finding is that the share of gains that went to labour went to the very top of the distribution of wage and salary incomes.
>
> (2005: 77)

In past two decades, US workers saw no measurable improvement in their wages, while US executives enjoyed the experience of suddenly becoming multi-millionaires. This is hardly a recipe for an equitable, well-integrated or orderly economy and society, and in this performance and reward culture, it is not surprising that the US now has among the worst social and health problems of any advanced industrial country and has rediscovered the scourge of widespread absolute poverty.

The elaborate structures designed to link executive reward to performance has often compounded problems rather than alleviating them, and too often CEO compensation is not due to achieving results but has amounted to rewards for failure (UK Trade and Industry Committee 2003). Essentially the extraordinary elevation in executive reward that occurred in the 1990s (and has continued since) in the US had little to do with the productive efforts of the executives themselves and was fuelled by the longest-running bull market in history. The sustained rise in share prices in this period reflected institutional savings flows and momentum investing, together with falling interest rates. Stock options became an accelerator mechanism providing risk-free bonuses to senior management.

> Corporate governance in the 1990s operated against a background of rising share prices, the capital market was not an agent of discipline but a facilitator of painless general enrichment through rising share prices; amidst increasing confusion about what management could do in a world whose stock market was running on narratives (not discounted cash flows) and encouraging CEOs to pose as heroes ... Many CEOs in the decade of the 1990s profited personally from using the language of value creation to cover the practice of value skimming.
>
> (Erturk et al. 2004)

When companies do use objective criteria for setting CEO compensation, these criteria are not designed to reward managers for their own contribution to the firm's performance, as bonuses are typically not based on the firm's operating performance or earnings increases relative to its industrial peers, but on metrics that cannot distinguish the contribution of industry wide or market wide movements. In fact, conventional stock options allowed executives to gain from any increase in stock price above the grant-date market value, even when their company's performance might have significantly lagged that of their peers.

There is a real danger that the excessive compensation secured by US executives is becoming the benchmark for executive reward in other regions of the world where up till now executive rewards have remained modest in comparison, and executive have pursued a balanced set of corporate objectives rather than their personal remuneration. The out-of-control inflation in executive pay in the United States threatens to impact upon executive reward internationally, beginning with the UK where CEO salaries were a small fraction of US CEO salaries until 1998 when a sharp and sustained inflation in CEO pay in the FTSE 100 occurred. In the past, there was some resistance to this as business executives in Europe and Asia were less enamoured to the short-term orientations of the U.S. counterparts, and identified with the sustained success of the companies they led rather than celebrating their own reward.

However, more European and Asian executives now look upon swollen US executive salaries as a benchmark to aspire towards. Already a higher proportion of executive pay is being offered in equity-based compensation and in incentive payments in other parts of the world, which were significant stages in the acceleration of the inflation of US executive pay. It may be questioned whether executive performance pay should be in the form of stock options at all since these create an incentive for management to manage performance of financial results in order to maximise share price. Pay for performance in the form of bonuses might better be linked to the underlying drivers of performance that impact on the financials, and to non-financial performance indicators in a more balanced scorecard. The focus could then be upon management for sustainability, rather than short-term performance management aimed at the stock price (Clarke 2016a).

The Reform of Executive Pay

As the inflation in executive pay has continued for several decades, interrupted, but not ended, by the corporate crises of 2001/2002 and the global financial crisis of 2007/2008, the public outcry against this manifest inequity and the calls for radical reform have increased to a crescendo internationally. Addressing the structural inequalities that Atkinson et al. (2011) and others have clearly identified will take a major overhaul of individual and corporate taxation, and significant repair of social, health welfare, and educational systems. However, the inflation in executive pay, which is the most public of the present inequities, has attracted a raft of specific reform proposals.

Often these proposals have proved idealistically conceived and widely popular, but either have been delayed in their introduction due to corporate resistance or remain in development. However, the reform movement on executive pay is now so broad some measure of success in restraining unwarranted increases may result. The US Institute for Policy Studies has outlined a number of principles for an improved CEO pay system.

Encourage Narrower CEO-Worker Pay Gaps

Extreme ratios between executive and employees pay run counter to principles of fairness and endanger enterprise effectiveness and commitment.

Eliminate Taxpayer Subsidies for Excessive Executive Pay

Taxpayers should not have to pay for the excesses of executives, and yet do so on government contracts which subsidise this life-style, and in corporate tax deductions.

Encourage Reasonable Limits on Total Compensation

The greater the short-term incentives for executives, the more temptation there is to make reckless decisions rather than pursue the long-term success of the company.

Bolster Accountability to Shareholders

An irony of the shareholder value movement is that the inflation in executive pay it has induced was achieved while disenfranchising shareholders, and boards answerable to shareholders are more likely to be more careful in justifying compensation they award to executives.

Extend Accountability to Broader Stakeholder Groups

Pay reform for executives should encourage executives towards decisions that take into account the interests of all corporate stakeholders including consumers, employees, and communities (IPS 2014).

As the Institute for Policy Studies (2014) records, there are many statutory and regulatory initiatives deriving from the *Dodd-Frank Act* (2010). They include measures intended to mandate disclosure on executive pay of the ratio of the median total annual compensation of their employees and the CEO; to disclose the relationship between executive pay and corporate financial performance; to disclose whether companies have a policy on executives hedging on their stock options (that is using hedging contracts to bet against their own firm's success, meaning that they will benefit if the company does well or not); to allow the right of shareholders to a non-binding vote on the compensation of executives; to allow shareholders to place candidates on the ballot for boards of directors; and finally to require securities exchanges to set listing standards related to the independence of board compensation committees and their advisers.

Of these measures, the greatest struggle to have the rule passed occurred with disclosing the ratio of CEO pay to median employee compensation, as the SEC admitted having passed the rule on 5 August 2015:

> As required by Section 953(b) of the Dodd-Frank Act, today's rules would require a public company to disclose the ratio of the total compensation of its chief executive officer ("CEO") to the median total compensation received by the rest of its employees ... The Congressional mandate under Section 953(b) has proven to be one of the most controversial rules that the Commission has been required to undertake under the Dodd-Frank Act.
>
> (SEC 2015)

This will mean major corporations will need to publicly reveal how much they value the efforts of all of their employees relative to the contribution of the CEO. Yet opponents of the rule mounted bitter opposition to this reform.

Internationally a campaign has continued against the trend to adopt the inflated US executive remuneration which is gradually spreading. In Switzerland, there was a popular initiative to limit executive pay to no more than 12 times worker pay, which was blocked by a massive corporate advertisement campaign. In the UK, shareholders now have a binding vote on executive compensation in public companies, and in the European Union, the internal market commission is proposing a vote on the ratio between the lowest- and the highest-paid employee in the company. In 2011, Australia gave shareholders the right to spill the board of directors if the executive pay report gets a "no" vote of 25 per cent or more for two consecutive annual general meetings. In France, President Hollande capped executive pay at firms where the government has a majority stake at 450,000 euros, approximately 20 times the minimum wage, and introduced a special corporate tax equal to 75 per cent of any individual executive compensation they pay over 1 million euros. All of these measures are contested and highly problematic in terms of application, but they do serve to focus further public attention on the outrage of unrestrained executive reward.

It is likely that this international campaign to place a restraint upon executive pay will continue; however, whether the trend towards endless inflation of executive reward will be stemmed is in some doubt, and will require a major political campaign to be effectively and continuously developed in policy and implemented in practice. Though these various attempts to restrain executive pay have merit, the efforts at reforms have to be placed in the context of the insistent trend of inflation of executive reward in recent decades, and the apparent capacity of executives to evade all restraint on the increase in their relative shares of the wealth generated by the enterprises they control (and the concomitant excess distribution to shareholders). It is not likely that any of these attempts to limit executive pay will succeed in any sustained way unless reform is associated with a substantial reformulation of corporate law, a radical redesign of corporate and personal income taxation, and a range of social and welfare reforms as occurred in the social democratic reconstruction following the Second World War. In the contemporary political world, which is almost as dominated by neo-liberal thinking as is business, such sweeping reforms are remote. There are some indications though that corporations and executives are realising they have to be seen to exercise more convincing social and environmental responsibility.

References

Atkinson, A.B., Piketty, T. and Saez, E. (2011) Top Incomes in the Long Run of History, *Journal of Economic Literature*, 49 (March): 3–71, http://eml.berkeley.edu/~saez/atkinson-piketty-saezJEL10.pdf

Bebchuk, L.A. and Fried, J.M. (2005) Pay without Performance: Overview of the Issues, *Journal of Applied Corporate Finance*, 17(4): 8–23.

Blair, M. and Stout, L. (2001) Director Accountability and the Mediating Role of the Corporate Board, *Washington University Law Quarterly*, 79: 403.

Blair, M.M. (2012) In the Best Interests of the Corporation: Directors' Duties in the Wake of the Global Financial Crisis, in T. Clarke and D. Branson (eds.), *The Sage Handbook of Corporate Governance* (pp. 62–80), London: Sage.Breeden, R.C. (2003). *Restoring trust: Report to the Hon. Jed S. Rakoff, the United States District Court for the Southern District of New York*, on Corporate Governance for the future of MCI, Inc. Inc. Corporate Monitor, 44.

Cadbury, A. (2002) *Corporate Governance and Chairmanship*, Oxford: Oxford University Press.

Clarke, T. (2013) Deconstructing the Mythology of Shareholder Value, *Accounting, Economics, and Law*, 3(1): 15–42.

Clarke, T (2016) *The Widening Scope of Director's Duties: The Increasing Impact of Corporate Social and Environmental Responsibility*, Seattle University Law Review, 39, 2, 557–602.

Clarke, T. (2017) *International Corporate Governance* (p. 720), London and New York: Routledge.

Clarke, T., Gholamshahi, S. and Jarvis,W. (2019) The Impact of Corporate Governance on Compounding Inequality: Maximising Shareholder Value and Inflating Executive Pay, *Critical Perspectives on Accounting*, 63, September, 1–17.

Clarke, T. (2020) The Contest on Corporate Purpose: Why Lynn Stout was Right and Milton Friedman was Wrong, *Accounting, Economics and Law*, 10(3): 1–46

Clarke, T. and Boersma, M. (2017) The Governance of Global Value Chains: Unresolved Human Rights, Environmental and Ethical Dilemmas in the Apple Supply Chain, *Journal of Business Ethics*, 143(1): 111–131.

Davis, G.F. (2009) *Managed by the Markets: How Finance Re-shaped America*, Oxford: Oxford University Press.

Deakin, S. (2005) The Coming Transformation of Shareholder Value, *Corporate Governance: An International Review*, 13(1): 11–18.

Dew-Becker, I. and Gordon, R.J. (2005) *Where Did the Productivity Growth Go? Inflation Dynamics and the Distribution of Income*, Washington, DC: Brookings Panel on Economic Activity.

EPI (2015) Economic Inequality, http://www.epi.org/research/economic-inequality/.

Erturk, I., Froud, J., Johal, S. and Williams, K. (2004) Corporate Governance and Disappointment, *Review of International Political Economy*, 11(4): 677–713.

Friedman, M. (1962) *Capitalism and Freedom*, Chicago, IL: Chicago University Press.

Froud, J., Haslam, C., Johal, S. and Williams, K. (2000) Shareholder Value and Financialisation, *Economy and Society*, 29(1): 80–110.

Hickel, J. (2017) Is Global Inequality Getting Better of Worse? A Critique of the World Bank's Convergene Narrative, *Third World Quarterly*, 38(10): 2208–2222.

Huse, M. and Gabrielsson, J. (2012) Board's Contribution to Strategy and Innovation, in T. Clarke and D. Branson (eds.), *Sage Handbook of Corporate Governance* (pp. 233–251), London: Sage.

IPS (2014) 2014 Executive Pay Reform Scorecard, Institute for Policy Studies, http://inequality.org/2014-executive-pay-reform-scorecard/

Ireland, P. (2005) Shareholder Primacy and the Distribution of Wealth, *The Modern Law Review*, 68(1): 49–81, Pew Research Centre, Washington, DC.

Jensen, M. and Murphy, K.J. (1990) Performance Pay and Top Management Incentives, *Journal of Political Economy*, 98(2): April: 225–265.

Lazonick, W. (1992) Controlling the Market for Corporate Control: The Historical Significance of Managerial Capitalism, *Industrial and Corporate Change*, 1(3): 445–488.

Lazonick, W. (2009) *Sustainable Prosperity in the New Economy: Business Organisation and High-Tech Employment in the United States*, Kalamazoo, MI: Upjohn Institute.

Lazonick, W. (2012) In the Name of Shareholder Value: How Executive Pay and Stock Buy-Backs Are Damaging the US Economy, in T. Clarke and D. Branson (eds.), *The Sage Handbook of Corporate Governance* (pp. 476–495), London: Sage.

Monks, R. and Minow, N. (2001) *Corporate Governance*, Oxford: Blackwell Publishing.

Parkinson, J. (2003) Models of the Company and the Employment Relationship, *British Journal of Industrial Relations*, 41(3): 481–509.

Piketty, T. (2014) *Capital in the 21st Century*, Boston: Belknap Press of Harvard University.

Porter, M.E. (1992) Capital Disadvantage: America's Failing Capital Investment System, *Harvard Business Review*, 70(5): 65–82.

Redmond, P. (2005) Companies and Securities Law: Commentary and Materials, Thomson Lawbook, Sydney: LBC.

Reich, R.R. (2016) *Saving Capitalism: For the Many, Not the Few*, New York, Vintage.

SEC (2015) Improving Transparency for Executive Pay Practices, Securities and Exchange Commission, https://www.sec.gov/news/statement/improving-transparency-for-executive-pay-practices.html

Stout, L. (2012) *The Shareholder Value Myth*, San Francisco, CA: Berrett-Koehler.

Tridico, P., & Fadda, S. (2018). Inequality and uneven development in the post-crisis world. Routledge.

UK (2006) *Companies Act 2006*, UK Government, https://www.legislation.gov.uk/ukpga/2006/46/section/171

UK DTI (2000) Company Law Review Steering Group, *Modern Company Law for A Competitive Economy: Developing the Framework*, UK Department of Industry.

UK House of Commons Trade and Industry Committee, *Rewards for Failure*, Sixteenth Report of Session 2002–2003.

UK Trade and Industry Committee (2003) *The White Paper on Modernising Company Law*, Sixth Report of Session 2002–2003.

Weinstein, O. (2012). Firm, Property and Governance: From Berle and Means to the Agency Theory, and beyond. *Accounting, Economics and Law: A Convivium*, 2(2): 1–57.

Weinstein, O. (2013) The Shareholder Model of the Corporation, between Mythology and Reality, *Accounting, Economics and Law: A Convivium*, 3(1): 43–60.

Wolf, M. (2002) Why It Is So Hard to Fix the Flaws of Modern Capitalism, *Financial Times*, November 20.

5 The *Social Licence to Operate*

Redefining Purpose and Fiduciary Duty

In *The Shareholder Value Myth* (2012), Lynn Stout demonstrates how an unfortunate lacuna in corporate law was filled by the simplistic tenets of agency theory, which has promulgated enduring myths of shareholder primacy that have been misconstrued as authentic legal interpretations of directors' duties, and often guided directors with increasingly narrow and damaging corporate objectives. The tenets of shareholder value are portrayed as eternal, universal, and unarguable. Lynn Stout resoundingly and convincingly exposes the multiple fallacies of each of these claims concerning shareholder value: the ascendancy of the claim of shareholder primacy (though it may have been stated in the past) is of comparatively recent origin in the agency theory wave in neo-classical economics of the late 1970s (Jensen and Meckling 1976; Henwood 1997).

Equally, the claim to universality of agency theory is bogus, since it is very much an Anglo-American construct, that for a long time was regarded as an alien intrusion into forms of European and Asian corporate governance (while it has now more influence in these regions due to the scale and power of Anglo-American investment institutions, shareholder primacy is still questioned on serious grounds of morality and practicality in most regions of the world (Clarke 2016; Clarke and Boersma 2017). Similarly, the critique of the basic principles of shareholder value has remained widespread and robust in the Anglo-American world (Lazonick 2012; Weinstein 2013; Clarke 2014).

The mythology of shareholder value has proved one of the most debilitating ideologies of modern times. The pursuit of shareholder value has damaged and shrunk corporations, distracted and weakened managers, diverted and undermined economies, and, most paradoxically, neglected the long-term interests of shareholders. It was in this period that the Anglo-American corporation was crudely translated from a wealth- and welfare-creating vehicle for the wider

DOI: 10.4324/9780429294648-5

community of stakeholders and whole economy, with an emphasis on the importance of all corporate resources, including the capabilities and training of employees, into a bundled portfolio of assets with the sole purpose of benefiting shareholder interests.

Experienced corporate managers with deep knowledge and capability in the business were replaced during this period with managers from outside the company drawn from finance, disconnected from the business units but focusing on financial markets and results. Holding companies came to control many formerly independent companies (Weinstein 2012). Lynn Stout discusses these "toxic" consequences of the maximisation of shareholder value alienating employees, customers, suppliers, and communities (Stout 2013, 2016; Clarke et al. 2019).

Finally, Lynn Stout insists that the "relentless focus on raising the share price of individual firms may be not only misguided but harmful to investors" (2012: 7). It is the ultimate irony that maximising shareholder value is so misguided it damages the interests of all stakeholders and may be ultimately especially harmful to the interests of long-term shareholding investors. In fact, agency theory reifies and misrepresents shareholders just as badly as it misunderstands every other stakeholder in the business enterprise. Lynn Stout offers a more balanced and accurate assessment of the composition and orientations of the ultimate shareholders:

> If we stop to examine the reality of who "the shareholder" really is – not an abstract creature obsessed with the single goal of raising the share price of a single firm today, but real human beings with the capacity to think for the future... and to make binding commitments, with a wide range of investments and interests beyond the shares they happen to hold in any single firm, and with consciences that make most of them concerned, at least a bit, about the fates of others, future generations, and the planet.
>
> (Stout 2012: 6)

The unravelling of the doctrine of shareholder primacy and the potential abandonment of the maximisation of shareholder value as the central driver of US corporations does now appear, to a degree at least, to be occurring in slow motion (Clarke 1998, 2015). The growing emergence of the *Social Licence to Operate*, the open debate on the *Purpose of the Corporation* (a company's fundamental reason for being), the revision of the core principle of the US Business Roundtable around corporate responsibility, and interest around the world in redefining the social and environmental obligations of corporations in the context of the devastating potential impact of climate change suggest the absolute reign of shareholder primacy is coming to an end (Clarke 2007, 2016; Veldman and Jansson 2020).

The widespread scepticism concerning aspects of what purports to be corporate social responsibility in the past can lead to rejection of the viability of the concept (Fleming and Jones 2013), and revelations of the extent of greenwashing undermining the corporate commitments to sustainability (Gatti et al. 2019; Netto et al. 2020), might suggest approaching new initiatives in this space with some caution. But what is impressive presently is the number and quality of initiatives around the world, coalescing in the United Nations *Sustainable Development Goals*. All this is occurring in the context of the dawning realisation of the desperate consequences of climate change for the economy and society if concerted action by governments, corporations, and communities is not taken quickly.

The Social and Environmental Responsibility of Business

The gradual emergence of the concept of the *Social Licence to Operate* instead of "business as usual" (BAV), beginning with the extractive industries (that were facing increasing difficulties with local communities where they intended to dig new mines) and extending now to the finance sector and other critical business sectors, is one indication of an incipient potentially seismic shift in business responsibility. It is difficult to be serious about a *Social Licence to Operate* while conforming to the wickedest tenets of maximising shareholder value (despite what Friedman said about "The Social Responsibility of Business Is to Increase Its Profits"). As the Social License gains traction, the demonstration of corporate social and environmental responsibility becomes more exacting (though remains still to be closely defined and measured):

- The *Social Licence to Operate*, or simply social license, refers to the ongoing acceptance of a company or industry's standard business practices and operating procedures by its employees, stakeholders, and the general public.
- *Social License to Operate* is created and maintained slowly over time as the actions of a company build trust with the community it operates in and other stakeholders.
- In order to protect and build social license, companies are encouraged to do the right thing, and then be seen doing the right thing (Kenton 2019).

Maintaining the *Social Licence to Operate* is becoming embedded in business purpose, as it is coming to be recognised as a strategic risk in which corporate legitimacy, credibility, and trust are in the balance. Corporations, as with other institutions, cannot function effectively for long without legitimacy, credibility, and trust. The *Social Licence to Operate* resonates with the traditional relationship-based approach to business in Europe, and the modern interpretation of the *Social Licence to Operate* is accepted widely by corporations throughout Europe and the UK. Now with the US Business Roundtable's new declaration of corporate purpose, the social license will be considered by more large corporations in the US (Autenne et al. 2018; British Academy 2018; Business Roundtable 2019; Clarke 2020). The social license is central to a new OECD initiative on *Trust in Business*, and appears to resonate with business internationally, and to relate closely to the United Nations *Sustainable Development Goals* (OECD 2019; UNEP 2020).

A significant indication of this change in business mood was BlackRock CEO Larry Fink's 2019 Letter to CEOs of the thousands of companies around the world in which BlackRock is a lead investor, in which he sets out the principles of the *Purpose of the Corporation*:

- Every company needs a framework to navigate this difficult landscape, and it must begin with a clear embodiment of your company's purpose in your business model and corporate strategy.
- The purpose is not a mere tagline or marketing campaign; it is a company's fundamental reason for being – what it does every day to create value for its stakeholders (Fink 2019).

A primary criticism of stakeholder capitalism is that any purpose other than shareholder profits results in a lack of focus and, can lead to corruption. This critique logically follows from the view that CEOs can be self-serving arbiters of social value and would, if given the opportunity, divert resources to their own enrichment under the guise of "purpose." In his 2019 letter to CEOs, Larry Fink disagrees with this assumption, stating in bold lettering:

> Purpose is not the sole pursuit of profits but the animating force for achieving them. Profits are in no way inconsistent with purpose – in fact, profits and purpose are inextricably linked.
>
> (Fink 2019)

Since BlackRock is the largest investor in the world (and reached $10 trillion in assets under management in January–October 2022), there was every reason for the CEOs of the thousands of companies that BlackRock is invested in, to sit up and listen. The question is whether this is largely a significant change in rhetoric being called for, or whether more substantive changes in business objectives and practices are being demanded? An important test case of this question is the apparent sudden about turn of the US Business Roundtable from a conservative shareholder value commitment held for some years to a more inclusive stakeholder capitalism perspective in 2019.

US Business Roundtable: *The Purpose of the Corporation*

The US Business Roundtable represents among the largest corporations in the US and has tended to reflect and propagate the dominant business sentiments of the time. In 1981, adopting an expansive view of corporate purpose the Business Roundtable stated:

> Corporations have a responsibility, first of all, to make available to the public quality goods and services at fair prices, thereby earning a profit that attracts investment to continue and enhance the enterprise, provide jobs, and build the economy ... That economic responsibility is by no means incompatible with other corporate responsibilities in society.
>
> (Business Roundtable 1981:12)

However, by 1997 the Business Roundtable had swung around into the Friedman shareholder primacy view, and sharply narrowed its focus to delivering shareholder value:

> The principal objective of a business enterprise is to generate economic returns to its owners ... If the CEO and the directors are not focused on shareholder value, it may be less likely the corporation will realize that value ... In the Business Roundtable's view, the paramount duty of management and of boards of directors is to the corporation's stockholders; the interests of other stakeholders are relevant as a derivative of the duty to stockholders. The notion that the board must somehow balance the interests of stockholders against the interests of other stakeholders fundamentally misconstrues the role of directors.
>
> (Business Roundtable 1997: 1, 3)

Then in the context of increasingly apparent environmental threats, new corporate regulations are being proposed in the US Congress pursued by Elizabeth Warren, Bernie Sanders, and others, and alarmed by an increasing public perception that corporations were essentially self-interested that President Trump did little to dispel, in a slightly stunning press release from their 2019 meeting in Washington the US Business Roundtable engaged in a very public *volte-face*:

> **US Business Roundtable Redefines the Purpose of a Corporation to Promote "An Economy That Serves All Americans"** (19 August 2019)
>
> Press release: WASHINGTON – Business Roundtable today announced the release of a new *Statement on the Purpose of a Corporation* signed by 181 CEOs who commit to lead their companies for the benefit of all stakeholders – customers, employees, suppliers, communities and shareholders.
>
> Since 1978, Business Roundtable has periodically issued *Principles of Corporate Governance*. Each version of the document issued since 1997 has endorsed principles of shareholder primacy – that corporations exist principally to serve shareholders. With today's announcement, the new *Statement* supersedes previous statements and outlines a modern standard for corporate responsibility.

This announcement of "a modern standard for corporate responsibility," and the accompanying analysis received front-page coverage in the US national press, and international media. "The American dream is alive, but fraying," said Jamie Dimon, chairman and CEO of JPMorgan Chase & Co. and chairman of Business Roundtable.

> Major employers are investing in their workers and communities because they know it is the only way to be successful over the long term. These modernized principles reflect the business community's unwavering commitment to continue to push for an economy that serves all Americans.
>
> (Shareholder Value Is No Longer Everything, Top C.E.O.s Say, *New York Times* 19 August 2019)

"This new statement better reflects the way corporations can and should operate today," added Alex Gorsky, chairman of the board and CEO of Johnson and Johnson and chair of the Business Roundtable Corporate Governance Committee. "It affirms the essential role corporations can play in improving our society when CEOs are truly committed to meeting the needs of all stakeholders" (*New York Times* 19 August 2019).

The shift from a shareholder primacy to a stakeholder rhetoric was adroitly handled in the press as a legitimate and rightful progression (when it was arguably a rhetorical return to the business values of the Roosevelt-Kennedy era) which might have caused some consternation among some sections of activist shareholder ranks if they thought it was serious. However, the fact that the new statement of stakeholder principles was agreed by 181 CEO members of the Business Roundtable, including leading captains of US industry such as Tim Cook of Apple, Jeff Bezos of Amazon, Larry Fink of BlackRock, Brian Moynihan of Bank of America, and Mary Barra of General Motors, provided conviction to the Roundtable statement that few in the media were prepared to contest. There were 181 CEO signatures attached to the new *Statement on the Purpose of a Corporation* (Business Roundtable 2019) which stated:

> Americans deserve an economy that allows each person to succeed through hard work and creativity and to lead a life of meaning and dignity. We believe the free-market system is the best means of generating good jobs, a strong and sustainable economy, innovation, a healthy environment and economic opportunity for all.
>
> Businesses play a vital role in the economy by creating jobs, fostering innovation and providing essential goods and services. Businesses make and sell consumer products; manufacture equipment and vehicles; support the national defense; grow and produce food; provide health care; generate and deliver energy; and offer financial, communications and other services that underpin economic growth.
>
> While each of our individual companies serves its own corporate purpose, we share a fundamental commitment to all of our stakeholders. We commit to:
>
> - Delivering value to our customers. We will further the tradition of American companies leading the way in meeting or exceeding customer expectations.
> - Investing in our employees. This starts with compensating them fairly and providing important benefits. It also includes supporting them through training and education that help develop new skills for a rapidly changing world. We foster diversity and inclusion, dignity and respect.
> - Dealing fairly and ethically with our suppliers. We are dedicated to serving as good partners to the other companies, large and small, that help us meet our missions.
> - Supporting the communities in which we work. We respect the people in our communities and protect the environment by embracing sustainable practices across our businesses.

- Generating long-term value for shareholders, who provide the capital that allows companies to invest, grow and innovate. We are committed to transparency and effective engagement with shareholders.

Each of our stakeholders is essential. We commit to deliver value to all of them, for the future success of our companies, our communities and our country.

(Business Roundtable 2019)

Except for the expressed belief in the free market system, it is likely that Milton Friedman would be far from happy at this remarkable statement of stakeholder capitalism principles by the leaders of US business. Critics of shareholder value might be amazed at the thoroughness of the stakeholder framework commitments that would not have been acceptable just a few years earlier to many CEOs who seemed now happy to sign up for them. From 1997 through to 2018, the Business Roundtable maintained a practice of issuing *Principles of Corporate Governance* which advocated the principle of *shareholder primacy* and relegated the interests of any other stakeholders as strictly "derivative of the duty to stockholders" (Posner 2019).

The Roundtable Statement was signed by 181 CEOs of Business Roundtable companies, but there were 241 CEOs in membership of the Roundtable in 2019, meaning 60 CEOs chose not to sign a document that would normally receive universal consent (and no reference was made to their views in the *Statement*). Questions remain to be answered regarding why the Business Roundtable should make such a comprehensive change in policy at this time, and about how viable in terms of translation into transformed operational values and practices is the US Business Roundtable's new vision of business purpose.

Besides the sharp jolt of Larry Fink's letter to all of them, the CEOs would be aware of a growing public sense of concern, and often anger, at the apparent indifference of big business to the complex social and economic problems insistently impacting upon, and disfiguring, the US (Clarke et al. 2019). Widespread under-employment, sustained low wages, extensive entrenched poverty, growing inequality, social and community break-down and environmental disaster within the US, and often even more extreme in the other countries and regions they operated in were no longer something large US corporations could readily ignore. As Martin Wolf put it:

The public at large increasingly views corporations as sociopathic and so as indifferent to everything, other than the share price, and corporate leaders as indifferent to everything, other than personal rewards. Judged by real wages and productivity, their recent economic performance has been mediocre. Furthermore, corporations have been allowed to corrode competition ... In short, bad ideas have seized the corporation and let competition waste away.

(*Financial Times* 12 December 2018)

CEOs now realised they had to appear as part of the solution rather than a significant cause of the problem and that this required an urgent recalibration of their public image if not their policies, which Jamie Dimon the chairman of the Business Roundtable was perceptive enough to see. The reality was that US business had fallen behind businesses from other regions of the world in their sense of commitment to corporate social and environmental responsibility, as indicated in a survey of CSRhub (2021). Both the American public and many of the CEOs themselves realised something need to be done according to recent surveys.

Purpose

Doubts concerning the social and environmental responsibility of US business will continue until there is solid evidence of action for change. There is some indication that some of the CEOs involved are becoming aware of these concerns. Representative views of the CEOs (US Business Roundtable 2019) included: Ginni Rometty, CEO of IBM: "Society gives each of us a license to operate. It's a question of whether society trusts you or not." Alex Gorsky, CEO, Johnson and Johnson: "People are asking fundamental questions about how well capitalism is serving society."

Views on whether the dramatic turnaround in the definition of business purpose by the Business Roundtable might have any practical utility were divided. The business academic community was generally supportive, but a little more exacting in their expectations. As Anita McGahan stated, "The focus on stakeholders is a focus on value creation. Managing for shareholder supremacy amounted to running businesses for their residual claimants rather than for sustained superior performance," and Meghan Busse:

A true broadening of the objectives of firms would improve the well-being of workers. But it remains to be seen how many of the CEOs who signed the statement are truly committed to making such changes, and also how many of them will and they are able to – given pressures from inside the firm, pressures from financial markets, and their own career ambitions.

(MIT 2019)

Concrete Commitments or Purpose Washing?

Alan Jope, the CEO of Unilever, in a prescient earlier statement emphasised not backing up purpose messaging could "further destroy trust in our industry" (Cannes, 18 June 2019). If all that results from the apparent *volte-face* of the Business Roundtable is a more accommodating rhetoric around stakeholder interests while still pursuing essentially the same financial metrics around maximising shareholder value (while neglecting all other stakeholders), the grand new Roundtable statement will be proven to be simply another exercise in *purpose washing* – cleaning up or disguising the essentially indefensible, while maintaining a consistent path of irresponsible business. Some critics have already dismissed the vague promises of the Business Roundtable as simply a clever new marketing exercise:

> The global reader may stumble over some of the phrasing, such as the commitment to a "free market economy that serves all Americans" – this from multinational companies with globe-spanning markets, outsourced operations and cross-border impact. We may also wonder how the announcement changes the workings of the free market in any discernible way. The weak pledges – to look after customers, to maintain good supplier relationships, to care for communities and the environment – could have been lifted from any one of the companies' existing annual reports. Employees at least get some specific assurances – fair compensation, benefits, training and education, diversity and inclusion – although of course the detail will be in the interpretation by individual companies. But communities and the environment, the most vulnerable of stakeholders, get the shortest, vaguest shrift in the statement. Communities will be "supported" and "respected" and the environment will be "protected" through sustainable practices. Clicking through on the Business Roundtable's website it is clear that the community and environmental investment that these companies have in mind is very much along the lines of the corporate-social-responsibility-as-charitable-giving that has proven extremely tax-efficient and brand enhancing in past years, without jeopardising any core profit centres. There is no commitment to engage with the harder, messier, more painful work of changing business

models to replenish currently abused and depleted communities and ecosystems.

(Meagher 2019)

Other sceptics of the new resolve of the Business Roundtable suggest this will not prevent more fundamental questioning:

> Whether or not the CEOs follow through on their pre-emptive nod to social responsibility, capitalism is clearly headed for a reckoning … Real-world experience has undermined free marketeers' near-theological belief that the unfettered pursuit of self-interest invariably produces the best outcomes for society itself. Banks' reckless pursuit of profits triggered the landslide of the 2008 financial crisis. Big Pharma made billions by creating an opioid epidemic that has ruined millions of lives. Fossil-fuel consumption is altering the planet's climate. The tech industry has seduced us all into surrendering terabytes of information that it sells at enormous profit. Executives cut themselves an ever-growing slice of the economic pie, while middle-class workers get crumbs. As they say on Wall Street, a correction may be coming.

(Falk 2019)

The Covid-19 global pandemic has provided a critical test bed for the renewal of corporate purpose. As recorded by the Test of Corporate Purpose (TCP 2020) initiative, the pandemic resulted in a profound economic crisis that exposed the multiple systemic fault lines around:

- wealth disparities
- ecosystem disruption that promotes novel virus incubation
- inadequate health care access and employment safety nets (TCP 2020: 6).

Though internationally corporations realised they had a role to play in this crisis, in the midst of the crisis, there was evidence of some companies "appearing to put profits ahead of people and shareholder expectations ahead of employees, communities and ecological well-being" (TCP 2020: 6). From the survey conducted by TCP (2020: 7), the following sobering conclusions emerged:

- BRT signatories did not outperform their S&P 500 or European counterparts on the test of corporate purpose since the inception of the pandemic.

- Companies with long track records of performance on corporate responsibility outperformed others.
- Proactive and substantive responses to the crises of the pandemic and inequality had the most impact.
- US and European corporations performed similarly.
- Shareholder capitalism is not fit for purpose in such crises, and new forms of alignment with stakeholders was required.

The Test of Corporate Purpose intends to continue research on whether corporations are delivering value to all stakeholders; on how employers have ameliorated or exacerbated inequality in terms of employee welfare and inequality; on the responsibility of capital allocation; on how governance integrates with other environmental and social commitments; on lobbying and political spending; and on taxes and tax havens (TCP 2020: 8–14).

Meanwhile, a preliminary analysis of empirical data regarding the declarations and performance of the Business Roundtable companies by Raghunandan and Rajgopal (2020) offers results that suggest there is a lot to be done. The 118 BRT signatories claimed that corporation purpose is to deliver value to all stakeholders rather than to maximise value for shareholders. Yet in a comparison of performance with industry peer firms:

- BRT corporations commit environmental and labour related compliance violations more often and pay more fines;
- Spend more on lobbying policy makers and receive more in targeted government subsidies.
- BRT CEOs receive higher abnormal compensation, and BRT firms have a smaller proportion of independent directors on the board (Raghunandan and Rajgopal 2020).

BRT corporations might claim they need more time to develop their commitments, but this is not a good place to start from. Exacting public scrutiny of how corporate performance matches policy declarations needs to continue.

If truly business is to demonstrate greater social and environmental responsibility, this must be reinforced by a positive and productive approach to practically resolving long-standing fundamental issues of corporate behaviour including:

- Commitment to compliance with relevant corporate regulation
- Acceptance of changes in directors' duties

- Agreement to pay a fair amount of corporate taxes rather than avoiding them
- Proportionate returns to shareholders relative to their equity commitment (Biondi 2012)
- Serious constraints and limits on excessive executive compensation
- Eradication of wholesale exploitation in global supply chains
- Acceptance of workers' rights
- Commitment to decent work and wages around the world, including in long supply chains
- Real commitment to product health and safety
- Commitments to environmental protection including net zero-emissions
- Pursuit of the circular economy

Corporations could be held to account for these more exacting standards regarding their purpose and performance, and there is required real evidence of a substantial shift in their commitments and practices.

References

Autenne, A., Biondi, Y., Cavalier, G., Cotiga-Raccah, A., Doralt, P., Haslam, C., Horak, H., Malberti, C., Philippe, D., Sergakis, K. and Schmidt, J. (2018) The Current Challenges for EV Company and Financial Law and Regulation, *Accounting, Economics, and Law: A Convivium,* 8 (3): 1–14.

British Academy (2018) *Reforming Business for the 21st Century,* Future of the Corporation. London: The British Academy

Business Roundtable (1981) *Statement on Corporate Responsibility,* Business Roundtable October 1981, Washington, DC, http://www.ralphgomory.com/wp-content/uploads/2018/05/1981-Business-Roundtable-Statement-on-Corporate-Responsibility-11.pdf

Business Roundtable (1997) *Statement on Corporate Governance,* Business Roundtable, September 1997, Washington, DC, http://www.ralphgomory.com/wp-content/uploads/2018/05/Business-Roundtable-1997.pdf

Business Roundtable (2019) *Statement on the Purpose of a Corporation,* Business Roundtable, Washington, DC, https://opportunity.business-roundtable.org/wp-content/uploads/2019/08/BRT-Statement-on-the-Purpose-of-a-Corporation-with-Signatures.pdf

Clarke, T. (1998) The Stakeholder Corporation: A Business Philosophy for the Information Age, *Long Range Planning,* 31(2): 182–194.

Clarke, T. (2007) The Evolution of Directors Duties: Bridging the Divide between Corporate Governance and Corporate Social Responsibility, *Journal of General Management,* March 32(3): 1–27.

Clarke, T. (2014) The Impact of Financialisation on International Corporate Governance, *Law and Financial Markets Review,* 8(1): March 2014, 39–51.

Clarke, T. (2015) The Long Road to Reformulating the Understanding of Directors' Duties: Legalizing Team Production Theory? *Seattle University Law Review*, 38: 437–490.

Clarke, T. (2016) The Widening Scope of Directors Duties: The Increasing Impact of Corporate Social and Environmental Responsibility, *Seattle University Law Review*, 39.

Clarke, T. (2020) The Contest on Corporate Purpose: Why Lynn Stout was Right and Milton Friedman was Wrong, Accounting, Economics and Law, 10 (3): 1–46.

Clarke, T. and Boersma, M. (2017) The Governance of Global Value Chains: Unresolved Human Rights, Environmental and Ethical Dilemmas in the Apple Supply Chain, *Journal of Business Ethics*, 143(1): 111–131.

Clarke, T., O'Brien, J. and O'Kelley, C. (2019) *The Oxford Handbook of the Corporation*, Oxford: Oxford University Press.

Falk, W. (2019) Is Greed No Longer Good? *The Week*, 23 August 2019, https://theweek.com/articles/860509/greed-no-longer-good

Fink, L. (2019) Profit and Purpose, Letter to CEOs, BlackRock https://www.blackrock.com/americas-offshore/2019-larry-fink-ceo-letter

Fleming, P. and Jones, M.T. (2013) *The End of Corporate Social Responsibility*, London: Sage.

Friedman, M. (1970) A Friedman Doctrine – The Social Responsibility of Business Is to Increase Its Profits, *New York Times*, 13 September 1970.

Gatti, L., Seele, P. and Rademacher, L. (2019) Grey Zone in – Greenwash out. A Review of Greenwashing Research and Implications for the Voluntary-Mandatory Transition of CSR, *International Journal of Corporate Social Responsibility*, 4 (6): 1–15.

Henwood, D. (1997) *Wall Street*, London: Verso.

Jensen, M.C. and Meckling, W.H. (1976) Theory of the Firm, Managerial Behaviour, Agency Costs and Ownership Structure, *Journal of Financial Economics*, 3 (4): October: 305–360.

Kenton, W. (2019) Social License to Operate, *Inestopedia*, 23 August 2019 https://www.inestopedia.com/terms/s/social-license-slo.asp

Lazonick, W. (2012) In the Name of Shareholder Value: How Executive Pay and Stock Buy-Backs Are Damaging the US Economy, in T. Clarke and D. Branson (eds.), *The Sage Handbook of Corporate Governance* (pp. 476–495), London: Sage.

Meagher, M. (2019) We Can't Rely on Corporations to Reform Themselves – We Must Challenge Power, *OpenDemocracy*, 26 September 2019.

MIT (2019) Will the Business Roundtable Statement Impact Workers? *MIT Sloan Management Review*, Strategy Forum, 25 September 2019, https://sloanreiew.mit.edu/strategy-forum/will-the-business-roundtable-statement-impact-workers/

Monks, R. and Minow, N. (2001) *Corporate Governance*, Oxford: Blackwell Publishing.

Netto, S., Sobral, M., Ribeira, A. and Soares, G. (2020) Concepts and Forms of Greenwashing: A Systematic Review, *Environmental Sciences Europe*, 32: 19, https://eneurope.springeropen.com/track/pdf/10.1186/s12302-020-0300-3

OECD (2019) *Trust in Business,* Paris: OECD, http://www.oecd.org/finance/oecd-business-and-finance-outlook-26172577.htm

Posner, C.S. (2019) So Long to Shareholder Primacy, *Harvard Law School Forum on Corporate Governance,* 22 August 2019, https://corpgo.law.harard.edu/2019/08/22/so-long-to-shareholder-primacy/

Raghunandan, A. and Rajgopal, S. (2020) Do the Socially Responsible Walk the Talk? https://ssrn.com/abstract=3609056 or http://doi.org/10.2139/ssrn.3609056

Stout, L. (2012) *The Shareholder Value Myth,* San Francisco, CA: Berrett-Koehler.

Stout, L. (2013) The Toxic Side Effects of Shareholder Primacy, 161 *U. Pa. L. Re.* 2003. https://scholarship.law.upenn.edu/penn_law_reiew/ol161/iss7/5

Stout, L. (2016) *Corporate Entities: Their Ownership, Control and Purpose,* Legal Studies Research Paper Series No. 16–38, Cornell Law School Science Research Network Electronic Paper Collection, http://ssrn.com/abstract=2841875

TCP (Test of Corporate Purpose) (2020) *Covid-19 and Inequality: A Test of Corporate Purpose,* Test of Corporate Purpose/KKS Advisers Reshaping Markets, https://c6a26163-5098-4e74-89da-9f6c9cc2e20c.filesusr.com/ugd/f64551_63f016a989db4dfeaa636d5a659d691a.pdf

Veldman, J. and Jansson, A. (2020) Planetary Boundaries and Corporate Reporting: The Role of the Conceptual Basis of the Corporation, *Accounting, Economics and Law,* 10(2): 75–88.

UNEP (2020) *Sustainable Development Goals,* United Nations Development Programme, https://www.undp.org/content/undp/en/home/sustainable-deelopment-goals.html#:D:text=The%20Sustainable%20Deelopment%20Goals%20(SDGs, peace%20and%20prosperity%20by%202030

Weinstein, O. (2012) Firm, Property and Governance: From Berle and Means to the Agency Theory, and beyond, *Accounting, Economics and Law: A Convivium,* 2(2): 1–57.

Weinstein, O. (2013) The Shareholder Model of the Corporation, between Mythology and Reality, *Accounting, Economics and Law: A Convivium,* 3(1): 43–60.

Wolf, M. (2018) We Must Rethink the Purpose of the Corporation, *Financial Times,* 12 December 2018.

6 Contemporary Challenges for Corporate Governance

Technological Transformation and Climate Change

Cycles of Governance

The cyclical historical saga of corporate governance revolves around the impulse of recurring historical waves of technological transformation impacting upon enduring agency and stewardship dilemmas of governance. Such dilemmas are universal in market systems, though internationally with different systems of corporate governance, the unwinding of this saga has occurred at different times for different reasons and with different consequences. Joseph Schumpeter made famous "the gales of creative destruction" that he believed was the essence of industrial capitalism (1994). The cyclical pattern of stock-market booms and busts caused by new technologies, innovations and opportunities, encouraging and concealing corporate excesses is recurrent through the centuries (Clarke 2022).

Complacency concerning the economic and social order reigns during confident times of business expansion, which, in turn, compounds the problems during the ensuing – and apparently inevitable – crises in corporate governance that lead to economic dislocation and social disruption. When recession brings increasing rates of corporate collapse, robust statutory intervention invariably occurs, often when it is already too late to avert disaster. Avoiding mandatory restrictive over-regulation requires active voluntary self-regulation through proficient governance – particularly in times of expansion. There will never be a "perfect" system of corporate governance. Market systems are inherently competitive and volatile and dynamic systems of governance will reflect this. Corporate governance is about risk management, and it is better to regulate to limit extreme irresponsibility than to bear the cost of repairing economic disasters. The drive to make corporate governance both improve corporate performance and enhance corporate accountability will continue. Balancing this tension between

DOI: 10.4324/9780429294648-6

performance and accountability is the key governance dilemma (Clarke 2022; Tricker 2023).

The *New Economy* in the US

The defining impulses of the late twentieth-century and early twenty-first-century corporate governance have focused upon the digital technological transformation that has seen the NASDAQ and other stock exchanges of the world dominated by technology platform corporations. With the renaissance of the digitally driven *new economy* in the US, the Anglo-American corporate governance system once again became generally regarded as the most robust. It was related to the largest economy, with the largest concentration of leading corporations, the deepest and most fluid capital markets, a dispersed shareholding base, and well-established laws and regulatory institutions, and in the early decades of the twenty-first century was regarded once again as possessing the winning formula.

> One of the strengths of the US system lies in its encouragement of self-regulation by corporate entities, supported by law around basic principles, but not mandated point by point. The US system enables people who know the corporation most intimately to effect its operation, so that the corporation can be positioned to achieve the highest level of efficiency and competitiveness it is capable of within its economic environment.
>
> (Millstein 2001: 10)

Just at the time it looked as if the American economy was about to enter a long period of gradual decline, much as Britain experienced a century earlier, suddenly the US staged a remarkable recovery. Reasserting its place at the forefront of the information technology, software, and media revolution, the US economy from the 1990s achieved higher productivity and sustained growth without a rise in the rate of inflation. As competitors in Europe and Japan faltered, the US was portrayed as a *new economy* with attributes that not only defied economics but confounded history, an economy that:

- grows without apparent threat of recession;
- continues to expand without increasing inflation;
- constantly restructures itself for greater efficiency and productivity;
- replenishes and revitalises itself through new technology and capital investment;

- functions without excessive debt, either public or private;
- maintains a balanced budget;
- increasingly becomes globalised and export-driven (Weinstein 1997).

There was much evidence that apparently supported this optimism (except with regard to the balanced budget): US competitiveness and productivity led the advanced economies; there was a faster expansion in industrial output than in any advanced country. The US appeared to have endorsed its leadership of technological advance and diffusion (OECD 2001d). This reinvention of the US economy created a sense of triumphalism that the US system of fluid capital markets and flexible labour markets was the most dynamic in the world. Silicon Valley became the envy of every country, with its clusters of energetically innovative high-technology companies producing the new software and technology the rest of the world apparently possessed an insatiable appetite for.

Despite warnings from the economist Paul Krugman and others that this sudden burst of productivity could be cyclical rather than permanent, the euphoria in the economy grew as hundreds of billions of dollars were invested in the apparently endless rise of the NYSE and booming NASDAQ, the world's largest electronic stock market. With apparently unlimited demand for new investment opportunities, telecommunications, computer hardware and software companies, and other high-technology firms experienced an unprecedented rise in their market capitalisation.

The economic significance of the increasing use and potential applications of internet technology was at the core of this industrial and investment revolution. A new knowledge- and information-based networked economy was becoming established, with the potential to capitalise on Metcalfe's law that as the scale of a network expands linearly, its use expands geometrically. This set the scene for the arrival of a horde of dot.com companies in the late 1990s which claimed in the prospectuses for their IPOs that the heavy internet traffic visiting their websites could readily be translated into burgeoning sources of revenue. Belief was suspended in the scramble to make serious money overnight in the dot.com revolution. It was this mentality that Alan Greenspan, chair of the Federal Reserve Bank of the US, famously dismissed as *irrational exuberance* (Shiller 2000). The scene was set for the biggest collapse in the NASDAQ and NYSE since the Wall Street crash of 1929 with the fall of Enron and WorldCom. Though the resulting regulation of the Sarbanes-Oxley Act was intended to restrain corporate America, the combination of sub-prime mortgages and toxic derivatives resulted in the financial crisis of 2008 that sorely damaged the global financial system. It was the euphoria associated with the derivatives traded on digital financial markets that erupted in the global financial crisis.

From Financial Crisis to Climate Crisis

The global financial crisis was a multidimensional, interconnected, and systemic crisis (Akerlof and Shiller 2009; Cohan 2009; Phillips 2009; Sorkin 2009; Clarke 2010; Johnson and Kwak 2010; Rajan 2010; Das 2011; Dunbar 2011). The G20 (Financial Stability Board), the IMF, the OECD, the European Union (De Larosiere Report), the US (Dodds– Frank Act), the UK, Australia, and other countries' analyses and prescriptions recognised this was a systemic crisis requiring systemic solutions. Among the causes of the crisis were international macroeconomic imbalances, institutional and risk management failure, corporate governance failure, and regulatory, supervisory, and crisis management failure. Understanding the compounding impact of these interconnected series of failures is the key to understanding the scale and intensity of the crisis.

Financial insecurity rapidly became contagious internationally as fears of a global economic recession became widespread and stock markets around the world crashed. This financial crisis was larger in scale than any crisis since the 1930s Great Depression, involving bank losses conservatively estimated in October 2008 by the IMF (2008) as potentially $1,400 billion, eclipsing earlier crises in Asia, Japan, and the US. Martin Wolf was quick to realise the implications of the crisis, as he put it in the *Financial Times* (5 September 2007):

> We are living through the first crisis of the brave new world of securitised financial markets. It is too early to tell how economically important the upheaval will prove. But nobody can doubt its significance for the financial system. Its origins lie with credit expansion and financial innovations in the US itself. It cannot be blamed on "crony capitalism" in peripheral economies, but rather on responsibility in the core of the world economy.

Relative to GDP, the financial sector in all of the industrial countries grew considerably in the past two decades of financial deregulation, innovation, and globalisation. The size of financial assets in both the US and the UK had more than doubled in 20 years. The massive growth of the UK finance sector and also the sustained growth of the European finance sectors involved the adoption of similar financial innovation and exotic instruments, as in the US. British and European financial institutions had also succumbed to the temptations of high leverage (in some cases higher than the Wall Street investment banks), minimal risk management, and a fascination with the returns that new financial securities and speculative industries – most notably the property sector – might deliver. In the UK, the financial sector became gargantuan, with assets around nine times GDP, a multiple more than double that of the US finance sector. A concentration on financial services was considered in the US and the UK as an essential part of the new economy, and was associated with rapid market growth, high profits and very high salaries for a privileged few dealing in the most exotic financial securities. Fuelling the whole process of financialisation were volcanic eruptions of debt.

As economies emerged from the global financial crisis, it was the platform technology companies that stormed the commanding heights of the NASDAQ, and Microsoft, Apple, Google, Facebook, and Tesla became the world's first trillion-dollar corporations (for Facebook (now Meta) and Tesla this proved a very brief experience). Similarly, in Asia, it was giant tech corporations (Tencent, Samsung, and Baidu) that appeared to be taking over. As the digital technologies of these corporations became infused in every aspect of economic and social life, these big tech companies appeared, briefly at least, to be invulnerable. Historically though, *Masters of the Universe* do not last forever, and each of the big tech companies faced increasingly concerned publics and governments as they morphed from engines of innovation and creativity to ones of monopoly and power.

While the economies of the world were still recovering from the global financial crisis, a systemic crisis of much greater significance was becoming apparent – 200 years of industrial activity in the name of *wealth creation* had seriously impaired the capacity of the earth to absorb the environmental impact. Pollution of the atmosphere by carbon dioxide and other greenhouse gases was causing global warming that was rapidly leading towards fatal damage to the ecology of the planet. This has suddenly presented governments and corporations with the imposing challenge to decouple economic activity from damaging environmental impact. The imperative of transforming towards renewable energy and other sustainable technologies resolutely and quickly demands a new green industrial revolution. Corporate governance aimed squarely at maximising shareholder value at whatever the cost to the environment has undoubtedly made a serious contribution to global emissions and to the dilemmas of climate change.

Business as usual is not a viable option. Businesses can succeed while exercising ethical values, respecting people and communities, and sustaining the natural environment. This requires comprehensive responsible policies, practices, and programmes fully integrated into business operations, incentive systems, and decision-making. The Global Compact defines corporate sustainability as "a company's delivery of long-term value in financial, social, environmental and ethical terms" (UN Global Compact 2015: 10). This is a good working definition for future endeavours.

Changing Paradigms in Corporate Governance

Contemporary corporate governance has evolved through a series of competing epoch-making paradigmatic contests. Tricker (1984, 2012) has suggested three distinct eras of corporate governance during which these contests have occurred can be identified:

- nineteenth-century entrepreneurship
- twentieth-century management
- twenty-first-century governance

In the nineteenth century, entrepreneurs advanced innovative new technologies and products, building businesses as enterprises they owned and controlled, and upon which they forged their own personalities and interests, often with great determination. As these enterprises increased in scale and complexity, there was a requirement for specialised management and additional investment beyond the means of the single entrepreneur. The call for external investment from dispersed shareholder led to the separation of ownership and control.

Though they existed from the beginning of the limited liability company, boards of directors became more firmly established in the twentieth century to pursue the best interests of the company and provide accountability for performance to wider shareholders. Often, however, the board remained nominally in control, and the incumbent executive management exercised effective control. In the twenty-first century, there is a demand for wider accountability and responsibility from businesses with the increasing recognition of the profound environmental and social impact of corporations. The UN and other international agencies have prompted national governments and business corporations to take action to reduce the damaging environmental and social impact of business activity, and a broad movement of investors and civil society have campaigned for more sustainable and responsible enterprise. Leading this movement are the vast investment institutions representing large sections of the community, including superannuation, insurance, and mutual funds. This has promoted a greater interest in the governance of corporations, and most recently in their sustainability.

Managers working in a specific era typically see the world through the lens of a powerful paradigm, encompassing frames of reference, metaphors, and perspectives which represent a degree of coherence, but which offer interpretations that often differ radically from those in use in preceding and succeeding eras. Paradigms are means of understanding the world, and the basis for informing action. The concept of paradigm is at once ancient and contemporary. Its name derives from the ancient Greek paradeigma. Classically, it meant a model or framework and this meaning has survived to the present day. It was a historian of science Thomas Kuhn who pioneered the idea of changing paradigms in *Structure of Scientific Revolutions* (1996). For Kuhn, science was characterised by the dominance of succeeding paradigms as models of thinking: "a constellation of concepts, values and perceptions and practices shared by a community which forms a particular vision of reality that is the way a community organizes itself."

While the idea of paradigms has been widely accepted in management studies, it has been more a contested than settled domain. In management, at any one time, there are a number of competing paradigms available (Clarke and Clegg 2000a). Using new frames of reference the managerial and organisational world not only looks different, it becomes different (sometimes presented as the social construction of reality) (Berger and Luckmann (1966). Paradigm shifts occur with a transformation from one paradigm to the next new paradigm. In these circumstances, during the period of transition, uncertainty and ambiguity will apply. Paradigm shifts are continuously challenging today because the pace of social, economic, and technological change is more rapid, and the impact of business on the environment and society is more profound. A combination of multiple technological breakthroughs, shortening product life cycles along global value chains, and rapidly changing markets are accelerating the pace of paradigm shifts, while serious questions are being raised concerning the sustainability of business enterprise (Clarke and Clegg 2000b).

The Evolution of Corporate Governance Paradigms

The evolution of corporate governance is shown in Figure 6.1 that highlights the different eras of governance, and the dominant theoretical and practical paradigms. As the contest between paradigms occurs over time, the reformulation of paradigms and the creation of counter paradigms takes place in a continuous dialectical tension of ideas with practice.

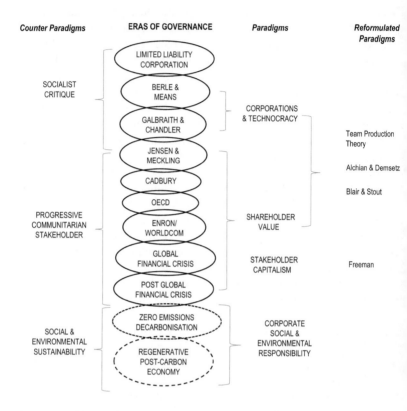

Figure 6.1 The Evolution of Corporate Governance Paradigms

The early decades of governance in the nineteenth century were spent wrestling with the implications of the limited liability corporation. In the 1930s, Berle and Means' (1933) recognition of the paradigm shift from owner-entrepreneurs to modern corporations with professional managers and dispersed shareholders defined the parameters of debate for the next half century, leading ultimately to the ideas of John Kenneth Galbraith (1952: 1967) and Alfred Chandler (1977) on the nature of the new industrial state and the managerial revolution during the expansionary years of the post-war recovery. In more troubled economic times in the closing decades of the twentieth century, the narrower focus of Jensen and Meckling (1976) on the principal-agency problem took hold with a vice-like grip on the minds of economists, lawyers, policy makers, and sometimes self-interested business people.

More recently a reform movement in corporate governance initiated in the 1992 UK Cadbury report, and disseminated internationally by the OECD, the World Bank, and other international agencies has continued, though defied by the spectacular corporate failures of Enron and WorldCom, and almost imploding in the recklessness of the global financial crisis, which led to the worldwide effort to regulate and constrain the excesses of the finance sector in the *Dodd-Frank Act* in the US, the Basel deregulations on capital adequacy and the governance of strategically important financial institutions, and many other international and national measures. Finally, there has been a widespread and insistent questioning of the sustainability of a carbon economy in the context of increasing pollution and global warming.

While this interest in corporate social and environmental responsibility was deflected in the urgency of restoring financial stability following the global financial crisis, it is these profound questions of the impact of corporations upon social and environmental sustainability that will preoccupy the paradigmatic contests of corporate governance throughout the remaining decades of the twenty-first century. To meet the imminent challenge of social and environmental sustainability in a post-carbon economy, further rethinking of corporate purpose, corporate governance, and directors' duties will be essential. This sustainability revolution has only just commenced, but in the course of the twenty-first century will transform business and society.

References

Akerlof, G. and Shiller, R.J. (2009) *Animal Spirits: How Human Psychology Drives the Economy, and Why It Matters for Global Capitalism*, Princeton, NJ: Princeton University Press.

Berger, P.L. and Luckmann, T. (1966) *The Social Construction of Reality: A Treatise in the Sociology of Knowledge*, New York: Doubleday & Company.

Berle, A.A. and Means, G.C. (1933) *The Modern Corporation and Private Property*, North Ryde: Commerce Clearing House.

Chandler, A.D. (1977) *The Visible Hand, Managerial Revolution in American Business*, Cambridge, MA: The Belknap Press of Harvard University Press.

Clarke, T. (2023a) *The Purpose of the Corporation*, Cambridge: Cambridge University Press.

Clarke, T. (2023b) *International Corporate Governance*, London and New York: Routledge, 2007; Third Edition.

Clarke, T. (2022) *Corporate Governance: Cycles of Innovation, Crisis and Reform*, London: Sage.

Clarke.T. (2010) *Recurring Crises in Anglo-American Corporate Governance, Contributions to Political Economy*, Oxford: Oxford University Press, 29(1): 9–32.

Clarke, T. and Clegg, S. (2000a) *Changing Paradigms: The Transformation of Management Knowledge for the 21st Century*, London: HarperCollins Business.

Clarke, T. and Clegg, S. (2000b) Management Paradigms for the New Millennium, *International Journal of Management Reviews*, 2(1): 45–64.

Cohan, W.D. (2009) *House of Cards: How Wall Street Gamblers Broke Capitalism*, New York: Allen Lane.

Das, S. (2011) *Extreme Money: The Masters of the Universe and the Cult of Risk*, New York: Portfolio.

Dunbar, N. (2011) *The Devil's Derivatives*, Brighton, MA: Harvard Business Review Press.

Galbraith, K. (1952) *American Capitalism: The Concept of Countervailing Power*, Boston, MA: Houghton Mifflin Company.

IMF (2008) *Global Financial Stability Report: Financial Stress and Deleveraging*, Washington, DC: International Monetary Fund.

Jensen, M.C. and Meckling, W.H. (1976) Theory of the Firm, Managerial Behaviour, Agency Costs and Ownership Structure, *Journal of Financial Economics*, 3(4) October: 305–360.

Johnson, S. and Kwak, J. (2010) *13 Bankers: The Wall Street Takeover and the Next Financial Meltdown*, New York: Pantheon Books.

Kuhn, T. (1996) *Structure of Scientific Revolutions*, Chicago, IL: University of Chicago Press, Third Edition.

Millstein, I.M. (2001) The Evolution of Corporate Governance in the United States – Briefly Told, *Forum for US_EU Legal-Economic Affairs*, Rome, Italy, September 12–15: 1–22.

OECD (2001) *The New Economy: Beyond the Hype: The OECD Growth Project*, Paris: OECD.

Phillips, K. (2009) *Bad Money: Reckless Finance, Failed Politics and the Global Crisis of American Capitalism*, New York: Penguin.

Rajan, R. (2010) *Fault Lines: Hidden Fractures Still Threaten the World Economy*, Princeton, NJ: Princeton University Press.

Schumpeter, J. (1975) *Capitalism, Socialism and Democracy*, New York: Harper.

Shiller, R. (2000) *Irrational Exuberance*, Princeton, NJ: Princeton University Press.

Sorkin, A.R. (2009) *Too Big to Fail*, New York: Allen Lane.

Tricker, R.I. (1984) *Corporate Governance*, Aldershot: Gower.

Tricker, R.I. (2023) *Corporate Governance*, Oxford: OUP.

UN Global Compact (2015) *Guide for General Council, 2015*, https://www.un globalcompact.org/library/1351

Weinstein, B.L. (1997) Welcome to the New Economy, *Perspectives*, 12(2): 1–4.

Organisation Index

Index